DAISY THE DUMPSTER DOG

A SORDID TALE OF DYSTOPIAN HUBRIS AND CONVENIENT CANINE RATIONALIZATIONS (BUT NOT A SUPREME COURT SATIRE OR MOCKERY OF OBEDIENT ORIGINALISM)

BLADE CORT

DAISY THE DUMPSTER DOG
Copyright © 2022 by Blade Cort

All rights reserved. No part of this publication or any elements from it may be reproduced, distributed, or transmitted in any form or by any means, including photocopying; recording; digitization or tokenization of characters, scenes, or any other components; or other electronic or mechanical methods without the prior written permission of the publisher, except for brief quotations embodied in critical reviews and certain other noncommercial uses permitted by copyright law. Permission requests should be provided electronically to the publisher.

This book is a work of fiction. Names, characters, businesses, organizations, places, events, dialog, and incidents either are the product of the author's imagination or are used fictitiously. Any resemblance to actual persons, living or dead, events, or locales is coincidental. References to any products or services are not an endorsement and are only intended to develop storyline and context.

First Edition September 2022

DAISY THE DUMPSTER DOG

A SORDID TALE OF DYSTOPIAN HUBRIS AND CONVENIENT CANINE RATIONALIZATIONS (BUT NOT A SUPREME COURT SATIRE OR MOCKERY OF OBEDIENT ORIGINALISM)

EPISODE 311 – DAISY

"ARE YOU A DOG?"

Daisy was immediately off-put by such a question. It's not like it was the first time she'd heard it. In fact, she was constantly teased by Nemmie's buddies who hounded her and her friends every day at the dumpsters. But they didn't matter, at least not at this moment. What did matter was that this sniveling, no-good chihuahua half-breed had the gall to ask her such a question. After all, he wasn't much to look at himself. Perhaps well-below 'much.'

She waited to bark a retort, knowing that such an indignity and personal slight must not be countered instantly or impulsively. No, she had learned her lessons from what seemed like years of taunting by other canines. She knew to pause until he was thoroughly full of himself; until he was certain he had firmly gained the upper hand and could therefore elevate his position above her in The Caste, the local hierarchy of dog dominance. Once this prickly-haired half-pint had become so captivated with his own ecstatic and sarcastic vinegar, so disengaged from reality, then she'd lunge for his jugular. Figuratively, anyway. She'd slay him with her calm wit and wisdom, disarm him with a word or two about where she stood in the broad scheme of things, and remind him how lowly his own status would be as a low-bred newbie at the trash bins.

Then along came another yapping barrage. "I asked if you were a dog, oh magnificently dull one. Did you get that? Do you have even the slightest capacity to respond to such a plain and simple inquiry?"

Daisy stared at him without twitching an ear or batting her long, white eyelashes, and waited patiently for more.

"I sense no tail to speak of," he continued. The mongrel moved his head side to side in order to glimpse her backside, as if she was curling it under her. "Quite disturbing. Clearly no tail. I see a little stump or stumpette or odd, boil-like growth on the ill-defined bum. Doubt that it's waggable, though. It's looking pretty unnatural to me, by all accounts, and is readily distracting to us real dogs."

At this juncture, Daisy's blood had begun to stir. Her front paw was slightly shaking in anger, sending a subtle signal to this mangy rat that she was about to bluster forth with her own cannonade of yelps. The impertinence of this pathetic creature, so quick to comment on her tail - or lack thereof. This entire encounter was a first for her. Shocking. She contemplated biting him, though a quick peek at his sniveling snout full of teeny, sharp teeth sent a signal that he might hold a few nasty tricks in abeyance.

Still receiving no response to his inquiries, he sighed. "Hey, I'm only asking an obvious question to an abundantly obvious omission, right? And any normal canine would assume that with such colossal ears, you should be super-enabled to hear me properly. My heavens, though, are those truly ears? They look like alien antenna designed to capture and relay a signal to attack our planet. Yeah, that's the correct conclusion about those unsightly obtrusions. You're an alien hybrid, but they forgot to hybridize in a tail to make you appear like a real dog. As if that wasn't bad enough, they engineered your ears way too large for the size of your head. Kind of donkey-like. No, I stand corrected. Jackass-like. And I can't determine what breed they intended you to be, either. Possibly an unfortunate mix between a wire-haired terrier and a Westie, if one had to guess. Either way, it's apparent that whatever those aberrant appendages are atop your skull, they're certainly not ears."

He took a few wary steps towards her, thinking she was indeed alien or maybe not even a dog. Worse yet, perhaps she had no commu-

DAISY THE DUMPSTER DOG - A SORDID TALE OF DYSTOPIAN HUBRIS AND CONVENIENT CANINE RATIONALIZATIONS

nications skills whatsoever. He'd known that type among many of his peers. Canines who had been abused so thoroughly by standies, those two-legged dogs, that they lost all ability to communicate except for occasional sad and forlorn whimpers. 'Those standies; what a waste of space,' he thought. 'One or two might be okay, a few indifferent, and most bad, at least in my experience. Never met one I liked much, and they didn't seem to appreciate my own stunning attributes, either.'

"You haven't peeped a word yet, whatever you are – alien, jackass, stub-tail dog faker," he mused. "I repeat: you're a dog faker. You likely don't even have a name, do you?"

Daisy's mind was churning wildly with comebacks. 'When should I interject? When is the optimal moment to slay this annoying dragonelle? I mean, look at the doltish dung beetle. An immobilized front leg, and it appears there's no fur under it. Maybe it's a defective robotic attachment? The insignificant imp has some nerve talking to me like this when it's clear he can hardly walk straight. He'll learn who's the boss around here when I embed a few Daisy toothmarks in his overstuffed butt.'

She also was sizing him up, wondering what pack to put him in. Clearly not her own pack. Hers was a tight team already, and he seemed far too annoying as an addition, should he stay. He would only drag them down and definitely diminish their status in The Caste. But given his pathetic limp, it was a greater likelihood that this newcomer was not transiting far from her digs; her lair. He might be sticking nearby for a while, at least until Nemesys and his gang of thugs showed up, so she needed to carefully consider a response. It was always better to make a friend than an enemy, she understood, even a friend as disgustingly mouthy as this one.

She could simply ignore his bluster and let him continue whining on this impotent tirade, making wisecracks about her appearance like he was a sit-up comedian verbally assaulting a patron that failed to laugh at a bad joke. But she was not about to laugh. In fact, she was so upset at this short-haired runt that both of her front paws were now visibly quaking.

He continued, confident that he could throw any insult her way without fear of a counterattack. "Geez. I'm getting nothing here. No tail. Excessively large ears. Alien. Then your front legs are overextended for your body. Do you realize that? They're taller than your back legs. If a saddle was placed on you, the rider would slide right off the back. Reminds me of pictures of hyenas that I've seen before. Yeah, maybe that's it. One of your near ancestors was a hyena. Problem is that you got none of their good traits, and the only unfortunate one that you did inherit makes your front legs appear too extended for your unsculpted, adipose-dense body."

That was it. She'd heard enough from this pipsqueak, and it was time to silence his itty-bitty toothy voice hole.

She began her witty retort by doing what she always did when confronted with trouble, at least the non-threatening kind. She lifted her top lip to expose her canine teeth.

"That's a pretty pathetic smile or attempted growl," he smirked ungraciously after surveying her mouth. "You should consider visiting a dog mouth standie about that tartar buildup, or you're bound to lose the rest of your front teeth."

"Darn wimp!" she whispered, sensing that she had accidentally exposed too much of another of her many obvious faults: the missing front teeth. She couldn't remember exactly how it happened, only that it did happen. One day, she was playing rope toy tug-of-war with her best standie mate, and he slung her in circles a bit as they played. Next thing she knew, her front gums were in pain, and she was forced against her will to visit the white-coated, dog mouth standies dude with the needles. Initially, she thought it would be just a fun ride in that box with wheels, yet it turned out instead as a bad trip for all. Fun jumping in and out of the box. Fun sniffing the grounds – until she was forced inside the big box to unwillingly confront those needles and pliers.

DAISY THE DUMPSTER DOG - A SORDID TALE OF DYSTOPIAN HUBRIS AND CONVENIENT CANINE RATIONALIZATIONS

But that was long, long ago. Water under the bridge. Things were great then. Nothing to worry about. Good food. Air conditioning and heat. A little box of her own to sleep in. Standies to play with. Nice ones. Felt like a family. Like being a part of something bigger and better, and far, far different than living the dumpster life. After fruitless searching, she'd given up on ever finding that great standies family. So, she returned to the life she knew as a pup.

The backyard gate blew open that fateful day, the day of the dark storm, and she decided to take a sniff around the neighborhood, outside the fence. But the sniff turned into a rout when that dreadful stray came at her with all fours in gear. She ran miles and miles it seemed, fleeing from that slug of a dog. Wet and tired, but in one piece, she attempted to trace her way back. Tried to locate her best standies ever. But it was as if they had disappeared. They and the big boxes they lived in. Indeed, it seemed the whole, entire neighborhood where she took walks had simply vanished. Nothing was the same despite endless searching. Exhausted and dejected, however, she found one silver lining. That dorco sign. It saved her. Every dorco had dumpsters, and that meant food and drink and smelly stuff to roll in and ingest. Dumpsters were the best thing that standie canines ever created for stray, four-legged canines.

"What? Did you actually squeak?" he howled with laughter, confident that he had one-upped her and elevated himself a few rungs. Things were appearing to start out well for him in these new surrounds, he considered.

She drew back at this latest slight. Couldn't he tell that with her ears, she had the best hearing in the entire dorco area and perhaps in all of dogdom? And his own ears were no walk in the park, either. Proportionately, they were almost as big as hers. Or maybe not.

"Shush," she hissed. "Watch that wicked tongue there, you ratty boy."

He looked around, first to his right, then to his left, as if unfazed by her weak attempt at a defensive counter. "Did you say, 'ratty boy?' Sorry, but is there another canine in the vicinity? I don't see one. Surely, you're not calling me that name? Me, a purebred chihuahua?"

EPISODE 312 – RAT DOG

DAISY RAISED HER NOSE high in the air.

That was the sign, wasn't it? The sign of complete disregard for any dog that stood before her. The ubiquitously recognized, subtle indication of indifference that was always spoken without speaking: 'Look, I don't know who you are, and I don't care about your presence. I smell a thing of far greater importance, and it's not you. It's off in the air, and you're not clever enough, or perhaps your olfactories are not advanced enough, to catch a scent like I can.'

She grumbled a response: "You're no purebred; that's clear. I'd say you're more rat terrier, which is the lowest of low breeds. Everyone should be familiar with the first law of hierarchical dogma. Rat terriers are below chihuahuas on the scale, which themselves are hardly mentionable in these parts without everyone rolling wildly in fits of laughter. On second glance, you're more likely a mongrel mix of both of these dreadful dregs. Ugh! Observe your pathetic, underwhelming being. Have you ever encountered your reflection? Has anyone ever described how you appear to their eyes? Don't you realize that you're a hybrid? And I don't mean 'high bred' or 'highly bred' or a hybrid canine that was bred for a loftier purpose. No, I imagine you were shamefully birthed for a lower purpose, such as using your acerbic tongue to entertain superior breeds like me that are much farther up on the hierarchy. Breeds who have important friends in high places. You, you little runt, are a rat dog. Some part chihuahua, some part rat terrier, and some part rat, if that's even possible these days."

He was surprised at her retort and having difficulty composing a reply, so she continued woofing her own tirade. "And I'm an expert at odd mixtures because I've seen hybrids of all kinds. A few standies have been up to no good for too long, combining us poor canines with more vicious mongrels like racoons. Using our DNA to create who knows what kind of weird anomalies. Why do you think we have a caste system, anyway? Do we really want to encourage your kind of mongrel mixes to stick around, much less multiply?"

He stopped her mid-stream. "Oh, then I suppose that's what happened to your tail, right? You're about to tell me that they cut it off when you were a mere pup, obviously enamored with how superior your innate genetic qualities were. And you'll claim that your tail, or what remains of it, is definitely sitting on the top shelf of a cryofreezer right now. That some very auspicious white-coated standie will occasionally extract it from that most revered and frigid place, sample a few cells from it, then use your ever-so-special genetic code to create the next wonder dog. Or possibly not 'dog' at all. Probably whatever in heck it is that you actually are, since I'm far from convinced that you have any genuine canine blood in you whatsoever. Not to repeat myself, but I'd go with jackass first, given the ears, and likely capybara since you lack a tail."

"Capy what?" she wondered.

"Geez, you nimbrain," he sighed. "Capybara. A large rodent with no tail. Their kind resides far away from this locale."

"Seriously? That's all you got? I'm afraid you are the rodent, Rat Dog," she chided. "Yeah, I prefer that name. It fits you well both in looks and attitude. I suppose you'll tell me that a standies family gifted you with an actual name like mine, which is 'Daisy,' as if it isn't obvious that I'm a perfect representative of that beautiful flower."

Rat Dog was weary from standing, especially since his front leg was not fully healed. He hobbled over to a soft spot on the dirt and sat down. "Don't tell me you've ever had a nice standies family. I truly doubt it. Not unless they were the white coat standies who accidentally invented you. But then, that's not a real family, is it? No, you clearly never had a family as I've had."

Since his comebacks were softening, she felt the conversation was finally beginning to flip her way. "I don't know you well, and I don't feel required to share anything personal with you. But I once had a great standies family. The best. Somehow, we got parted and I ended up here. And now that I've exposed the naked truth, I'm sure you'll tell me a sob story about how you were separated from your lovely standies family. And you'll wax on and on about how great they were and how much they adored you, until it comes to the part about your leg and how it ended up being so defective like that, and then your whole story will fall apart."

Rat Dog shook his head. He was tiring of inventing new invectives, and she clearly wasn't giving way to consider letting him in the local hierarchy via this verbal jousting. He was pretty sure he'd have to start at the bottom rung in this pack, which was the only rung he'd ever been at.

"Assuming you can handle the frightening yet true story, I broke my leg in a heroic jump," he bragged. "Shattered. It's in a cast. It's not a robotic leg, as if I was one of those AI dogs. Those are fake dogs, if you ask me. Fakers. I can't imagine why standies would want one of them."

Daisy tilted her head slightly to amplify the softball comeback. "Because they don't poop, they don't pee, and they don't eat. They're also smart and not the progeny of repugnant breeds like you."

"Whatever," he replied, as if he didn't care.

"And how did this leg get broken? You likely peed the floor for the umpteenth time, and your standies family complained that 'enough is enough.' Then they swept you out the door along with the rest of the trash. While you were in mid-air, the broom stick whacked that fragile toothpick you call a leg, and it snapped like a twig."

"No!" he cried. "You're totally wrong. I was always too fast to get hit by that dang broom. Dang that broom! There was the broom, and then there was the stick. Never took to the stick, and they always ran after me with them."

She smiled, feeling fully vanquished. "Because you peed repeatedly, or 'repeededly,' in their large box, I assume?"

"Bullcrap. You can't possibly know."

EPISODE 313 – TALE

RAT DOG HUNG HIS head down sullenly, recalling what had really happened.

They did use the broom on him. Too many times. They were never around to take care of him for even the basics that standies should do such as filling his bowl or setting out clean water. Too much into their own indecipherable babble and arguments and throwing things at each other.

He understood his one purpose for them, however. It was to bark at every noise, every wisp of air, because they were always scared, those standies. Scared that a thing was coming to get them, to hurt them, or to take their stuff. He was their early warning signal. That's all he meant to them. Never got petted. Always was teased and yelled at. That, and the broom, or the stick, or a barely warranted paw slap or boot on the rear.

'It hardens you,' he considered. 'Makes you grow up tough, though, or at least to talk a tough game. And in this new world of mine without such standies, you either elevate yourself with the other canines or get trashed by them.'

For her part, Daisy loved verbal jousting. No bites and no long-term injuries, just one-upmanship. And she could do that pretty well, despite her relatively small cranial walnut. "I'm sure you'll tell me a tall tale about that front leg, since the single asset you seem to possess is your tactless, tasteless, and torrid tongue."

"I jumped," he cried.

"Jumped? Jumped?" Daisy teased. Then she leapt high in the air which is what she used to do to get attention when the standies were sitting at the food ledge. "Jumped like this? Oooh! Ow! Look, I broke my leg bounding in the air. Oh, woe is me!"

"Not that kind of jump, Daisy. You know, that name doesn't suit you very well. Or better yet, it needs to be rhymed. Give me a moment to think. Crazy Daisy. Hazy Daisy. Lazy Daisy. Those are good starts. I'll come up with a better moniker and only need a few minutes to develop a rhyme to complement your fatuous, gratuitous, and acrimonious personality."

"Don't call me fat, you stinky rat. If I picked up any weight recently, it's because they've been loading cartloads of that stale bread and cake into the dumpsters lately. And hey, you're trying to change the subject. So, please continue your ineffective sob story about how you broke your leg jumping to rescue a baby standie. That you dragged it to safety from a flooding ravine, or pulled it off the tracks, or another sly and squalid tale."

He chuckled fiendishly. "Just a point, Lazy Daisy. You might consider extracting that word 'tale' from your limited vocabulary. It draws too much attention to your obvious lack of one."

Daisy shook her head in disgust. This conversation was going nowhere, and it was getting close to dinner. Her stomach was already growling. Besides, she'd need to secure suitable sleeping arrangements for the night. Probably under the hedges in her usual lair if no higher-ranked canines took dibs on it first.

Fearing that she was losing interest in his story, he continued. "As I said, I jumped. Not willingly, mind you. And not because I was trying to save anyone but myself."

"That figures," she concluded.

"There was a fire," he clarified. "The standies I stayed with lived on the second stacked box. That's one reason why I peed so often on their soft floor. They were too lazy to let me outside enough. I understand

DAISY THE DUMPSTER DOG - A SORDID TALE OF DYSTOPIAN HUBRIS AND CONVENIENT CANINE RATIONALIZATIONS

how to go outdoors. I get the rules. I was paper-trained. Then the stick. Or the broom. Or the shoe. I clearly got the message early on. I'm not stupid. Did I already mention that?"

"Maybe," she offered.

"But one night, the meanest standies guy lit a fire smoke stick in his mouth, and a few minutes later the soft cushion he sat on was aflame. In their haste to leave the box, one of the standies tripped over me."

"Sure," she replied, rolling her eyes in complete disbelief. "Please, continue yip-yapping, as this is one of the taller, um, uh, stories that I've ever heard from a short dog."

"You meant to say 'tales,' right?" he snickered. "You can't help yourself but to say that word since it's apparently so central to the core of who and what you are. Or aren't. Well, anyway, you'd have thought the oversized lugnut tripping over me might have broken my leg, but no."

"And I'm supposed to ask at this point, what, may I ask?" she queried.

"How my leg broke, Miss Witless."

"You already said you jumped," Daisy relayed. "I assume you got out of the way before your puny corpse was completely squashed by his paw?"

"Nice try," he replied.

"Is this imagined event also where you got that black eye from?" she giggled. "It appears as if the whole eye never healed properly. Permanently black, perhaps. Or maybe it's black atop that mangy white, short, stubble-crust hair, which I'd never call 'a real fur coat' like mine. The unfortunate mark covers a good chunk of that side of your face. Geez, that whack must have hurt, right?"

Rat Dog, too, was tiring of the repartee. Besides, most dogs rarely held a lengthy conversation with him. He was unimportant and uninteresting, and he knew it. "I'll not grace your comment with the effort of a reply. No, I won't. But I'll finish my story because it proves how I'm afraid of nothing. No thing and no canine."

"Except your own shadow."

He ignored her comment, feeling he had to finish the story before he lost her completely. "The fire was raging and encircling me. Flames were shooting at my rear, toasting my backside. Loud noises and crackling embers crashed beside me. The standies had already run to the ground, but I couldn't for obvious reasons."

"Which are?" she wondered.

He didn't think about what might come next after that comment flew from his mouth, because it would be a clear indication of how utterly incompetent he was to get along in the world. Certainly on his own, or maybe even with a standie who cared the slightest degree.

"The stairs were on fire," he claimed.

"The stairs? The stairs were made of wood? How old was this stacked box you all lived in?" Daisy asked.

"Not too old," he admitted.

She scanned the horizon with disinterest, as if waiting for a friend to pass by and relieve her from this small burden of verbosity. "Sorry, but I've visited many such places, the boxes stacked atop each other. I've navigated their stairs lots, in fact. My old best standie would take me there. He was a brother to me. He had a girl at one of the stacked boxes, one he visited a lot. But the stairs were made of that hard rock stuff. Not wood. Was it one of those places?"

"Yes," he continued, realizing his tale was now starting to show signs of being too tale-like. Of course, the real case was that the stairs were indeed made of the hard stuff, and they weren't on fire. He was just too pudgy to slide down them properly without rolling downward uncontrollably. Point of fact, he'd never successfully navigated a single stair during his brief life.

"Hey, quit interrupting with senseless questions," he demanded. "It's annoying, so let me finish. I was the last one in the burning box. I'm out on the front porch, staring way below at all the standies running everywhere. Flames are nipping at my tail, which as you can see, I

DAISY THE DUMPSTER DOG - A SORDID TALE OF DYSTOPIAN HUBRIS AND CONVENIENT CANINE RATIONALIZATIONS

carry in full, masterful regalia. The heat is unbearable and I'm preparing to die. Then, I notice a pack of red-suited standies on the ground. They're shooting water up towards me, but not enough to quench the fire. One of them called up to me. He said, 'Jump! Jump into my arms.'"

Daisy peered quizzically at him with eyebrows raised. "You're saying you understand the gibberish that standies make?"

"Yes, a little. So, I was left with little choice. It was either stay there and become charred dog bacon or leap courageously, far out into the abyss. My mind raced, as I knew I'd face certain death, even if the standies could break my fall. I hoped I might live for a brief moment thereafter to get a look at how far I had fearlessly jumped."

"And then?" she asked, feigning a wide yawn to indicate her boredom as well as to remind him of the size of her canines.

"My legs were much stronger at the time," he admitted, "and I sailed well over his head. I recall something touching me on the way down. A trace of a paw nail, perhaps. Then I woke up in the white-coat place with this lousy cast on my leg."

Annoyed that she had wasted precious moments listening to him babble, she was having none of his heroic explanation prattle. "That's it? You're telling me you were on the second stack of this box. That there was a fire nipping at your grotesque, immodest butt. That you had no other choice than to jump, so you did, and the red-suited standie waving below must have missed catching you. Then you woke up after this traumatic event, and the only thing that happened to you was that your front left twig there snapped? I mean, if you're gonna tell stories filled with big lies, please make them believable or humorous. You saw that I yawned constantly through this incredibly tedious narration. I'm just saying, if you want to hang with us in this place, you've got to do better than this. Certain of the higher ups in The Caste, as we call it here, are far less tolerant of aberrant and boring canines like you. I don't run things fully here, but I am fairly well thought of. Plus, my small pack and I hold our own decent position in the scheme of things and it's pretty high up there. You shouldn't go fibbing about everything to everyone. It comes off as desperate."

Rat Dog was silent for once, fearing that there was truth to what she said. "Patches," he blurted out.

EPISODE 314 – TAIL

"PATCHES? WHAT DOES THAT mean?" she asked.

"One of the standie families who had me, my first, called me that name. Not 'Rat Dog.' Just 'Patches.'"

"That's a dumb name," she woofed. "Patches. Was this before or after you got the big black eye?"

"You're not getting it," he lamented. "They called me that specifically because of the eye. As if I had a patch over that part of my face."

"Geez!" she exhorted, "Standies and their stupid naming. You mean you were born with this patch? Wow, living proof right there that some canines get none of the goodies."

"Then there were additional names," he confessed. "'Cutie Pee Handsome' was one. That was at the place with lots of dogs running around and barking constantly. Kept us caged. Could never sleep. Ever been there?"

Daisy thought back with trepidation. "Not that I recall, though I've been through a lot in my three seasons, and things are pretty easy to forget."

"Well, that was a bad name," he confided, "especially when a standies family took me from that place and I'd always poop and pee on their floor because they were too thoughtless to let me go outside. You don't go naming a canine 'Pee' anything. It just not right."

"I'll give you that," she agreed. "Were there more odious names?"

He pondered for a second. "The naming never seemed consistent from standie to standie. 'Flake' was one. I'm sure there were others."

"Yep," Daisy laughed. "The name I gave you fits far better than these, given what I've heard thus far. Of course, that could change depending on how flakey you turn out to be. So 'Rat Dog' is what we're calling you while you stick around this place. And you can pee wherever you want, mister Cutie Pee Not Handsome, which is a good thing."

Rat Dog stood up straight. After that 'Not Handsome' comment, he was not about to let this one go. "And you? I've divulged basically my entire life. All I've heard is that your name is Daisy and you're possibly part dog and unknown animal or alien, one with enormous ears and no tail."

"While we're being honest," she sighed, "I guess there were a few other names for me. Dixie. Stinky. Yeah."

"Stinky?" he laughed. "That's totally demeaning, and it's apparent you've suffered long-term psychological damage from such a moniker."

"No, not really," she answered, not catching the slight. "I always took my names as a sign of affection. Look, I've had a few bad standies, and I've had the best in the world. I'm okay with that. They can call me 'Twinkle Toes' if they want, as long as they're nice to me."

"Not so here," Rat Dog lamented. "Those two legged, standie dogs have been no friend to me, except the ones at that place where lots of us lived. That was great, though they were always barking and not sleeping."

"We'll talk more about that place later, as I am intrigued. For now, Rat Dog, I'll tell you how things work in this neighborhood. And my buds are due here before long, as it'll soon be time for dumpster Delights to arrive. These dorco standies are pretty consistent about delivering Delights. Oh, and if you're planning on staying very long, I'll need to get you fully initiated into the hierarchy of The Caste. Be aware that you'll start out on the lowest rung and probably never climb higher, given your ignominious breeding situation."

"Sounds stupid. Like a lame stage play. What is 'The Caste?'"

DAISY THE DUMPSTER DOG - A SORDID TALE OF DYSTOPIAN HUBRIS AND CONVENIENT CANINE RATIONALIZATIONS

Daisy was sorry she had brought it up. He didn't seem smart enough to understand. "Honestly, I'd rather cover that topic on a full stomach. Let's head over to the bushes and I'll show you a relatively safe place for us to stay tonight. Our lair. We'll emerge to catch the dumpster grub, assuming Nemesys and his buddies don't wolf it all down first."

EPISODE 315 – BADBOY

IT WAS LATE AFTERNOON and close to dinner. Daisy's stomach growled loudly.

"Can't you shut that annoying thing up?" Rat Dog complained after having made himself comfortable in the safe, shady space beneath the hedges. He settled into his new digs just fine, though Daisy made him move three times by warning him that the others in her pack already had secured those favored spots. Not having met them yet, he was none too pleased with this arrangement, and was forced to shift his chubby behind regularly to avoid the small branches hanging down that tickled his back.

"I don't understand why I can't choose my own spot in here," he continued. "It's not as if their names are painted up above these hovel pads. This should be a very democratic process. First come implies first served. No prior dibs allowed."

Daisy shook her head and stared disgustedly at him. He'd mouthed off considerably in the few hours she'd known him, and she wasn't certain if the rest of her small pack would allow him to stay. "I'm afraid your diminutive trap there will be no match for the bites that Dug or BadBoy can inflict on your hindquarters, once they get a taste of your vile windbags."

"Dug? BadBoy? What's the name of the third unfortunate in this pathetic mongrel mix of four?"

"You mean Dingo?" she questioned.

"Yeah, you failed to mention Dingo. Does he lack fangs or teeth? If so, then I'll be glad to accept his spot."

DAISY THE DUMPSTER DOG - A SORDID TALE OF DYSTOPIAN HUBRIS AND CONVENIENT CANINE RATIONALIZATIONS

Daisy raised her paw in caution. "Hold on, tiny toddler. Dingo could boot you a couple of hedge rows across the way with a swift flick-kick of his leg."

"Ooh," he shook in feigned fear, "must be a real charmer, this Dingo. Look, I've encountered muscle-bound hounds here and there, and I can easily run circles around them until their tongues are sagging and slagging on the ground. I fear no Dingo."

This was the mouthiest creature she had ever encountered, and she was getting tired of it. "Dingo's a robot dog, you naïve pup. Robotic. Doesn't need teeth because he doesn't eat." Then, hoping to shut him up, she bawled with emphasis, "You Rat Dog!"

His ears lowered instinctively, and he backed off, a telltale sign that he knew he was pushing it.

"Keep your lip-flapping, yip-yapping to a minimum, I suggest, if you're thinking about joining my group. Personally, I'm second guessing my decision to bring you into our lair because you do nothing to elevate our status in The Caste. I said before that you're an unholy, unfortunate mix of the two lowest breeds in the canine hierarchy. Better be on your best behavior and hope my friends are in good moods today, and that they'll allow you to at least stay the night. You don't want to be outside naked and alone with Nemesys and his gang of thieves and miscreants sniffing-up the place."

"Sheesh," Rat Dog shot back, seriously considering that he'd better get in touch with his gentler self for the upcoming introductions with her friends in the den.

Sometime later, Daisy was standing at the doorway of their lair, a small opening in the thick hedge, waiting for her friends to appear. "Ah," she surmised, holding her nose high in the air, "BadBoy is about to arrive."

"How would you know that?" Rat Dog inquired, barely lifting his head off the ground to take notice. "I don't smell anything."

"If your nose was slightly more substantial, your brain might pick up on these wonderful smells. But as they say in our world, 'Where the nose is inadequate, the olfactory intellect follows.'"

"Hey," he responded angrily, "I've been my sweet, quiet self the last few minutes. How dare you disparage me when I've been such an angel."

"Disper-what?" she asked. "Stop hacking your confusing words at me. My brain is primarily engaged in the most important thing in the world for canines. Scents."

"And my brain is used entirely for charming and cunning," he snapped back, "which means I'm not as limited in my approach to life as you. There's far more to understand than smelling, Daisy."

"And he's finally here!" she exclaimed, bounding upward happily at his arrival. "BadBoy, where have you been?"

BadBoy was no stranger to these parts. He was one of the longest-lived residents and had experienced the ebb and flow of migrations into and out of the local packs. Though he was purely mongrel, he imagined himself as a descendant of superior breeds. He appreciated Daisy's assessment of his bloodlines the best, as she mentioned this the first time they met.

'You're no mutt, that's for sure,' she told him at the time. 'I'd wager champion yellow Lab mixed with full-sized chocolate poodle. That's how you get your magnificent brown and gray coat. Then throw in a pinch of royal wolfhound, given your height.' He really took pride in that last part, 'royal' wolfhound, since he considered it among the most elegant and stately of all breeds. But it was only imagined. Either way, the two bonded instantly in that moment.

"What in tarnation are you?" Rat Dog spat, having lifted himself shakily onto all fours to establish a dominant position with the new arrival.

After his extended exploration trek earlier in the day, BadBoy was ready to assume his regular spot in their lair and rest for a bit. But this

DAISY THE DUMPSTER DOG - A SORDID TALE OF DYSTOPIAN HUBRIS AND CONVENIENT CANINE RATIONALIZATIONS

new blob of flesh was blocking the entrance. "Probably enough. And what are you?" BadBoy replied.

Shedding his short-lasting attempt to behave properly, Rat Dog started right in. "It's obvious what I am, so I won't grace you with an answer. Look, dude, you're too big to fit in here properly. Me and Daisy, we're normal-sized dogs, not a shaggy, unkempt monolith of super-mutt. Though I don't have much of a sense of smell, as I was just observing, do you have any capacity under that thick, matted tangle on your head to comprehend how sickeningly musty the whole area has become now that you've arrived?"

Rat Dog started shaking his forelegs and rolling his eyes in circles, as if he was about to lose consciousness. "Daisy, I'm not sure I can tolerate being around this guy. Is he for real? Is it possible for a dog to be so uncombed, so unclean, so unkept, that it makes every dog smell like heaven in comparison? If so, we've found that dog. Hallelujah, brother, we've finally found that dog!" He sniveled a minor laugh at the last comment.

BadBoy's head slowly began drooping as Rat Dog continued his nasty tirade. It was now so low that the hair on his ears was touching the ground.

Daisy had noticed this behavior too often from her old friend. "Hey," she urged, "don't let this bellowing muddled breed get you low, BadBoy. All he can muster in his pathetic arsenal of defense is this vile, insulting mouth, with no other meaningful or worthwhile features to speak of. He can't help but flap his wormy lips to excess. Don't let him affect you."

But Rat Dog was far from finished. "And where did you get this name of 'BadBoy,' huh? What nimbrain gifted you with that unfortunate appellation?"

BadBoy's head sunk lower. He raised his eyes toward Daisy, begging for help. And Daisy knew the truth, too. The whole, sad truth about BadBoy's past and how he was 'gifted' with that name.

"I confess," he began, in a deep, meager voice, "that I don't remember my real name. My former standies never used it, anyway. All I can ever recall was the name 'BadBoy' since that's what they repeated relentlessly. 'Did you make this mess on the floor? Bad boy! Did you turn over the trash can and eat these chicken bones? Bad boy! Were you sleeping on the bed again? Bad boy!' Life was an endless series of 'Bad boy' episodes, until I finally took refuge in the streets."

Before Rat Dog could mouth back, Daisy interjected. "BadBoy, he's a ratty nuisance and not worth the effort. But I'm so proud of you for having the courage to describe your painful past this openly. Think of it. At some point, you'll stop hanging your head low. At some point, that masterful tail of yours will come out from beneath you and stand straight up in the air, as it should."

Rat Dog couldn't help himself, and looked straight at Daisy, chuckling, "I've mentioned it before. You're not the one who should be talking about tails, as you're no expert in that area, obviously."

She ignored him, understanding that his snide remark was inevitable once the words left her mouth. "Come in, dear friend, and make yourself at home in your favorite spot. We're nearing the moment for dumpster Delights, and let's hope tonight's meal is a king's feast intended for a royal wolfhound such as you!"

At that mention, BadBoy stood up straight and raised his head proudly. His tail appeared momentarily to rise from beneath him, beyond the horizontal. "I imagine so," he replied happily.

After the exhausting exchange, the three rested in their places, hardly peeping a word for a few minutes. Rat Dog, however, always the energetic gasbag, felt uncomfortable in the silence. He was trying to be friendly.

"Hey BadBoy, perhaps during the next big rain, you and I can go for an extended walk outside. One that lets you kind of, you know, get washed off. I mean, you've got that long, matted hair. I can't make out what color it is. Brownish gray, I'd say, but that's also the color of dirt,

DAISY THE DUMPSTER DOG - A SORDID TALE OF DYSTOPIAN HUBRIS AND CONVENIENT CANINE RATIONALIZATIONS

which appears intricately embedded within your dreadlocks. Conversely, did you notice my own luscious coat? Did you see how well-cropped my hair is? Reminds one of a duck's feathers, and the rain easily slides off me. I'm naturally a clean, perfect canine machine. My friend, most are not as fortunate as me. Yet, I've seen instances where a stinky, disheveled dog like you can mitigate their horrific musty mess by simply taking a stroll in a good drenching. I'm sure doing that would make you more, uh, attractive to the girls and all."

BadBoy was lying down in his spot with his eyes half open. He was exhausted after chasing rabbits across the dry fields. Of course, he didn't catch one and wouldn't know what to do if he ever did. But the activity was fun, it didn't involve anyone else, and rabbits never insulted him. They just ran. "Sure," he grunted, trying also to be polite to this new and quite possibly temporary acquaintance. "Perhaps I'll take you up on the offer the next time water pours from the sky."

Right as he set his head back down, Daisy sniffed the air again.

"Dumpster delights about to arrive?" Rat Dog wondered, his beady eyes bulging out at the thought.

Growing tired of his annoyances, Daisy frowned. "I'll tell you when that's about to happen. In fact, you'll hear it from the commotion that occurs before the dorco standies appear outside. A real ruckus, that, given the lineup of canines waiting for the treats. No, my nose tells me that Dug is within sniffing range."

Rat Dog's impatience was palpable. "This is the kind of activity your mind is engaged in? Smelling the air to see who's coming or going? Can you imagine the amazing questions that rivet and rivulet through my mind at every moment, Daisy? Nah, I doubt you'd comprehend. Stuff like how we got here. Why the shift in light goes from day to night, and what the bright things are in the sky. And why are all these four-legged, non-canines around since they're boring and useless? Why don't standies look like us? Questions such as that. Imponderables. And while my mind is exploring the meaning of a dog's life and the universe in general, it's obvious that your own meager intellect is solely concerned with the next rotting smell or fetid dog passing by. One can only speculate how that poor walnut thrives within the oddly shaped, minuscule shell that is your noggin. Probably half of that shell's purpose is to keep your ears upright. I'm guessing the fragment of space that remains is for olfactory. In my book, olfactory is dull-factory, meaning you're utterly predictable and uninteresting."

"You sure talk a lot," BadBoy complained, opening his eyes slightly and scowling at Rat Dog. "Daisy, please tell me when Dug gets here, because her arrival means it's close to Delights. I want to be ready to go for it when the getting is good."

EPISODE 316 – DUG

A DOOR OPENED AT the back of the dorco and Daisy rushed out of the lair to take a look. "Geez, it seems a bit early for a Delights delivery," she mumbled. "The regulars haven't even arrived yet. Certainly not Nemesys and his scamps."

A standie, one of the regulars, held a twisted metallic contraption in his paws. He was wrestling with it, trying to lift the thing above his head. In one big grunt, he heaved it into the dumpster where it crashed against the back wall, making a terrible racket.

Because Daisy's oversized ears were able to pick up the slightest sound, she winced at the screech. "No need to get excited," she stated to the other two who hadn't moved from their spots. "Yes, it was a standie. He threw something in one of the dumpsters, but it wasn't the usual bags of Delights. It didn't look edible at all. No smell to it. Yet, it might signal that they're inside and preparing our feast."

"You'll let us know, then?" BadBoy inquired. "Except for that mouthy rat's continual lip-flapping, I'm half asleep and prefer no interruptions." Then he repeated, "Don't forget to wake me when the Delights arrive. Of course, we'll have to wait as usual for Nemesys and his cultish cowards to take first dibs."

At this remark, Rat Dog suddenly bolted up at attention. "What did you just say?" he yelped.

BadBoy's eyes were closed and he was already back to snoring, so Rat Dog quickly limped to the opening. "What did he mean by that?" he demanded.

"Mean by what?" Daisy replied.

"Smelly-guy's last comment. The one about 'taking first dibs.'"

She glared at him as if he was the most ignorant of the species. "I see you need to get educated about The Caste. The Caste. Don't you get what that implies? As it stands, you're already the lowest of lows, and my team, my pals, we're out there in the middle of the various packs who partake in Delights and such. But we're moving up, or we were indeed moving up until your unfortunate arrival."

Ignoring her slight, Rat Dog's front leg, the unbroken one, began to shake uncontrollably, and he started panting nervously. He was enraged and uncertain what she meant. This was his first time in an organized group of packs. He'd only ever been with standies, and this was all new to him. "Then you'd better tell me, or I'll be 'casting' my teeth into the hindquarters of every four-legged creature within range. I ain't afraid of nothing, as they say. The only cast that's relevant to me is the one on my leg here, the one I broke in a courageous, four-stacked boxes leap from a vicious fire."

"Four-stacked? I thought you said the box you jumped from was one stacked atop another. You're now suggesting that your chubby body floated like a butterfly down four of those stacks, and all you broke was your front leg?"

From behind the two, a raspy voice suddenly joined in. "Who jumped from a stacked box?"

Daisy spun around instantly. "Dug!" she screamed. "Where have you been?"

Dug backed away, given that Daisy's excitement often resulted in her jumping up high in the air and occasionally smashing paws when she landed.

"Calm down, girl. Daisy! Get ahold of yourself. We saw each other this morning." Dug then tilted her head to and fro, looking completely befuddled. "And who's this new ball of dandruff hanging out by our door? Some lowbrow visitor of yours?"

DAISY THE DUMPSTER DOG - A SORDID TALE OF DYSTOPIAN HUBRIS AND CONVENIENT CANINE RATIONALIZATIONS

Before Daisy could begin formal introductions, before she could issue a warning, before she could open her mouth and emit the first word, Rat Dog's brain had already devised dozens of snide remarks about this new arrival. He was certain this first criticism would immediately disarm the unwelcome visitor and place him in higher status, especially after he heard the 'lowbrow' comment.

"Which side of you is speaking?" he stated flatly, as if he was actually having difficulty assessing the problem.

Dug was taken aback by the comment. "What could you possibly mean?" she asked politely.

Daisy tried inserting her body between the two, knowing that Dug was unlikely to be as docile as BadBoy, once Rat Dog's epithets began. "Don't you dare mouth off to her!" she whispered to him.

He stood up on his fours to peer around Daisy, then overtly surveyed Dug's frontside and backside. "I mean," he insisted, "that it's not clear to me which end is speaking. Is your voice coming from the left side or the right? I see a few holes at one end, giving the dubious appearance of a nose. Maybe even an eye there. And both ends are covered with folds of skin so thick that nothing moves when you speak. Nothing. It's as if you have this unique ability to doublespeak, meaning from both ends. I'm asking as any logical dog would who's curious and friendly, such as myself. So, I'll ask in genuine kindness: From which end of your carcass do you speak, or is it both ends? Are you a circus dog who does tricks, perhaps, and they call you 'Doublespeak Dug?'"

Dug was not slow. Not at all. She had seen her fair share of scrapes along the way, many with mouthy bowsers like this one. Others with canines far larger than her. And she could hold her own with the Felinus residents as well. In fact, they gave her a wide berth after she'd proven her fighting prowess to certain aberrant individuals in that town. But this puny creature, he struck right at her heart of well-hidden self-doubt.

'Okay,' she'd admit to herself, 'so what if Dad was a half-breed, flat-nosed pug who bolted immediately after he had his short-lived tryst? So what if Mom was also flat nosed, but a purebred Shih Tzu? She had good bloodlines. Good ones. And I can't help it if I have a terrible underbite, or if my long fur is dingy brown. I can't help it if no standie has ever made the effort to comb my coat. And what's the big deal if my nose is flat, really flat, or that I'm brachycephalic with congenital snoring and occasional oxygenation issues? So what if I pass out when it's hot? I'm me. I'm the best version of me that I can be, and I'll use everything in my considerable powers to prove it. Nobody's better than me. Nobody. Every canine is just a mongrel breed with stories they tell themselves about why they're superior, when they clearly aren't superior in any respect. They're all simply dogs. I have nothing to hide and nothing to be ashamed of. I'm proud of who I am.'

But she had never run into a canine that possessed the utter social ignorance and vicious, creative genius to spew such abrasive comments. To think of it. She had just met this rat and he suggested that he can't tell whether her butt is her face, or her face is her butt. That was some gall, indeed! In her usual manner, she decided to approach the next exchange cautiously to size up whether he deserved a bite, which was a serious infraction in dogdom. Her mouth and jaw were definitely bigger than his, and she knew she could do substantive damage to the unmuscled twigs sprouting from his underbelly.

"Is that a broken leg I see?" she offered, trying to change the subject.

"Did you say the word 'see?'" he continued. "So, tell me how it is that you are actually able to see. You sport no eyes to speak of, so it's unclear which side they're on. And, by the way, is your secret to defending yourself similar to those fish in aquariums? You've seen them, right?"

Dug shook her head quizzically.

"Oh, come on," he persisted. "You must have noticed the orange fish with black dots on both sides of their body. When they're in the water, bigger fish who might eat them for lunch get very confused. The

DAISY THE DUMPSTER DOG - A SORDID TALE OF DYSTOPIAN HUBRIS AND CONVENIENT CANINE RATIONALIZATIONS

wanna-be predators can't determine whether the orange dot fish are coming or going, advancing or retreating, moving backward or moving forward. I'm guessing that same tactic must be your primary means of defense, given that both ends of your body look the same. And your carcass is probably really tiny beneath that matted fuzz, unless that's also part of the act. Maybe they bite into you and get this mouthful of foul-tasting, tangled fur. I bet they'd be puking hairballs for a few days after that!"

She was beside herself. 'What a horror of a dog,' she thought. 'I must respond in kind.'

"Daisy," she countered, "it would appear this new canine is the lowest of lows. Rat terrier mixed with chihuahua. Am I correct?"

Sensing it was now too late to warn Dug about his vile nature, Daisy shook her head in affirmation and shrugged her shoulders. "Sorry; I wanted to tell you earlier, but he beat me to the punch bowl."

"I can see why he acts this way, then," Dug continued, "given the low breeding or lack thereof. And no positive attributes overall."

Daisy surprisingly rendered a defense. "Don't you think you're being a little rough on the poor new guy?"

"Rough? Who said I was rough?"

"I think I just said it. Rough. As in 'rough rough.'"

Dug was slightly verklempt. "Me rough? Rough? I must speak. Being rough with this mouthy character is an art."

"Arf? Did you just say 'arf' or am I hearing things?"

"No. Use the antenna atop your cranium, dear one. Art. Not 'arf' as in 'arf arf' and not 'rough' as in ruff ruff. Daisy, are we just barking our heads off here?"

But Rat Dog was on a roll and not about to let that nominal rebuke interrupt the dollop of denigration gushing from his devious mind. "Psycho dribble from both of you. And Dug? Dug? Who gives a dog a name like 'Dug?' Of course, I can't smell so well. If I could, your scent would likely be masked too much anyway by that annoyingly wrangled and tangled tussle of spaghetti that you're wearing. Therefore, I feel obliged to ask outright. Are you a guy or a girl?"

Still jolted by this continual onslaught, she thought that confessing something about herself might change the tone of the conversation and get it to a friendlier level. "I'm a girl, of course. And my name? Well, my last standies called me 'Dug.' A result of me digging in the garden. They were not pleased with that, but then, they shouldn't have planted that stuff there for me to dig up. Besides, where else could I bury my bones? The ground everywhere was otherwise hard-packed."

"Then they rightfully booted you out the door?" he concluded.

"So to speak. In fact, Daisy is the only one I know whose standies were nice to her. Right, Daisy?"

She teared-up at the mention. "Right, Duggie."

"What's your story, dyspeptic newcomer? And what happened to that front leg of yours?"

"You don't want to hear it," Daisy assured her.

Rat Dog knew that this was his opportunity to boast again and perhaps raise his status. "If you have a few minutes, I'll tell you a harrowing tale about how I courageously leapt from six box stacks up, while a raging fire was blistering my butt."

Taking notice of a new commotion at the dumpsters, Daisy needed to cut the conversation short. "When he first told the story, he jumped from two big boxes. The number keeps increasing. But let's save that talk for later. Nemesys and his troupe of toadies have finally arrived, meaning that Delights are about to be delivered."

EPISODE 317 – NEMESYS

THE FOUR WAITED QUIETLY at the elevated dirt lip of the hedge, along with a cadre of dumpster dogs who knew to wait for their cue before daring to get closer to the action. Most of them watched in obedient awe as Nemesys and his gang pranced openly across a well-worn path from the dorco front lot toward the six-foot-high, scratched and rusted, faded blue dumpsters in the back lot. But a moment of quiet was all that three of them were allowed to enjoy.

"What the heck are we waiting for?" Rat Dog complained.

Nemesys, a muscular, black on brown and oversized Belgian, led the procession. He turned his head and frowned disapprovingly at the visitor's comment, as it was a clear breach of the dumpster ritual to allow anyone to bark anything until he and his lackeys assumed their rightful places, twenty paces in front of the dorco door. Even then, conversations were to be appropriately muted until the entitled ones had enjoyed their Delights.

"Hey, you dolt. Shush it!" Dug hissed, increasingly annoyed by this newcomer. "There's a process here, and you need to snap your trap shut until it's our turn to eat."

Rat Dog's head began swirling. He'd never heard of a 'process' when it came to eating anything. If the kibble was laid out there, you went for it. Laissez-faire. Sprang at it. No holds barred. Dove right in, hoping your speed could at least gain you that first, sweet mouthful. If tougher dogs then forced you out, you'd shimmy and slime and snap your way back in and hope you were quick enough to avoid their nasty nips. Process? The only process he knew was the 'dog-eat-dog' one he'd experienced since he made that fairly recent, heroic jump and was thereafter required to fend for himself. No longer did he have the assurance of occasional bowls of food or water supplied by his neglectful standies. Yeah, his situation had regressed.

'And that,' he rationalized, 'is why I've lost a bit of weight. Since the fateful leap, I've had irregular access to lousy leftovers from someone else's meal, assuming the cats and rats didn't get to them first. Nothing like the regular supply of fatty, gummy, chewy, gooey, nasty, rasty table scrap crap that my former standies would drop down, or a sip of spilled beer or sweet soda, my favorite. Worst case, it was eggshells or spilled flour on the floor, gagging it through the gullet with what little saliva I could muster.'

Nemesys finally sat at his vaulted place, with the small gang of favored followers taking their allotted seats in arrears. As they waited, all canines in the area, over twenty in total, began nervously stirring. Standing up. Sitting down. A few rolled on their backs as if warming up their bodies for the forthcoming joust over Nemesys' leftovers. Or maybe it was plain joy, imagining what was to come soon.

Rat Dog peered disgustedly at Dug's face. The poor girl was slobbering uncontrollably. Foam and spit slithered down her exposed jowls, making his stomach churn in disgust. Lowering his voice just enough to avoid further notice, he ignored Dug's counsel. "And who in the heck is this parade of mongrels that get first dibs at Delights? How do they rate over me?"

"Because they do, and they can," BadBoy whispered. Dug would have responded in kind, but she was too busy trying to lick the slobber off her cheeks and nose.

Daisy was ignoring them. She was far too smart to engage in useless chat when food was at stake. By now, she was a veteran of the process. All of it. The Nemesys ritual. The deference that the packs gave to him and his gang. The watchful waiting and tension that preceded the opening of the dorco door, the magic portal to a bellyful of Delights.

DAISY THE DUMPSTER DOG - A SORDID TALE OF DYSTOPIAN HUBRIS AND CONVENIENT CANINE RATIONALIZATIONS

After surveying the situation, she stood and walked in a half circle to face the three. "Don't anyone speak," she whispered to them.

"Hey, you're blocking my view!" Rat Dog complained.

"Quiet!" she demanded, and Rat Dog cowered in obedience.

"I don't want the others to hear this," Daisy confided, "but my ears tell me there's none of the usual activity on the flip side of the dorco door."

"No pawsteps from the standies?" Dug asked, her face contorted in fretful hunger pangs.

"None that I can tell," Daisy replied.

"And what in hell's canyon does that imply?" Rat Dog blustered aloud.

"I said to shut the clap trap!" Dug demanded. "You're getting noticed."

Nemesys had been sitting at attention in his usual spot, awaiting the forthcoming Delights, but his head spun around at this second outburst from the new arrival. He peered menacingly for a moment in their direction as if he was heading over to check out the noise, but then thought better of it given his proximity to the door and lateness of the Delights appearance. He sat down slowly, a signal that future unrestrained outbursts would meet his wrath.

Daisy's usually buoyant mood turned sullen. "You will quickly learn, Rat Dog, that the promised Delights are indeed that. Promised. Not certain. Intermittent. Not every day. Usually coincides with a lack of boxes with wheels in front of dorco. I saw very few out there today, and I'm guessing that means no Delights this evening."

Rat Dog was stunned so literally that for a moment, he was speechless.

"Looks like no dinner again for us poor canines," BadBoy whined, his head sagging. "I'm disintegrating into a whisper of dust."

"But on occasion they're late," Dug added hopefully. "We've seen before where they deliver Delights after the daylight fades. Perhaps it's happening again."

"I doubt it, Duggie," Daisy countered. "I hear none of the usual activities inside dorco, not the kind that leads to Delights. And the few times when they did come late in the day, it always coincided with lots of boxes with wheels out in the lot. I don't want to be the bearer of bad news to the packs, but my gut tells me we're out of luck for today, my compadres."

By now, Rat Dog had come to his senses. "Your gut? Your gut? What about Rat Dog's gut?"

"Dude! Shut your trap," Dug snapped. "Nemesys might hear you, and that would really shake things up."

"Indeed," BadBoy added. "Nemesys is never friendly, but he and his gang get far more agitated when Delights fail to arrive. Best to discreetly saunter away from here before they realize the bad news. Thankfully, Daisy's outstanding, oversized ears are the best for hearing the goings on behind the dorco door."

Rat Dog started to shake uncontrollably at the mere thought of missing dinner for a third night in a row. "All this prep. All your buildup and discussions about Delights, Daisy. And now you're suggesting that they're not going to appear? What kind of canine torture is this? A promised land of treats, patient waiting and politeness on my behalf during the entire day, then nothing to show for it?"

He was not about to take this sitting down. Gaining whatever ounce of courage he could muster, he stood up straight and headed directly down toward the vaulted, exalted positions near the dumpster. That one, the one where Nemesys and his gang sat in stillness, impatiently waiting for Delights.

His three friends pleaded in unison, "Come back! Don't do it!"

EPISODE 318 – BLISTER

RAT DOG HOBBLED FEARLESSLY toward Nemesys, who had no idea that he was approaching. The big dog was far too engaged in listening for a hint that the dorco door was about to open and provide the usual torn buckets and packages and cartons of Delights. Ambling slowly, given his broken leg, Rat Dog walked past Nemesys' number two, Blister, who was sitting a respectful distance away from his boss, as typical. Blister, a purebred, tan and white boxer with a black and white face, was salivating profusely from his oversized jowls, awaiting the promise of Delights. He hardly took notice of the pudgy, motley spotted, brown and white chihuahua-rat terrier mix that had just sauntered past him.

Despite his size, the thought of being second at anything always bugged the heck out of Rat Dog. He wasn't about to let a caste system or societal rules or customs or norms tell him what he could and couldn't do when food was in the offing. He also wasn't about to let anyone have first dibs at what might be coming. He'd seen and done important things in his short life, he recognized, and recently some very courageous things. Indeed. He jumped from a flaming box and nearly into a standie's waiting paws. He survived on his own for what seemed to be a long time. He even got rolled beneath a box's wheel, then sprang up from the mishap with nary a scratch or snap of the cast. But the potential of death, pain, and suffering? None of these were more urgent and meaningful to him than hunger. And hungry he was. Besides, no canine was better than him, though none were worse. They were all equal in his eyes, and no dog should be more or less entitled to Delights.

In his dangerously overconfident and ravenous mental state, Rat Dog quietly limped past Nemesys and sat in front of him, facing the dumpster. He settled his butt at the halfway point on the shortest line between Nemesys and the anticipated Delights. Somewhere during that short walk of both desperate clarity and uncertainty, Rat Dog had considered that, should things get dicey, he could play the 'injured dog' wildcard, or maybe the 'new dog' excuse. That he could talk his way out of any dangers resulting from this obvious boldness. No harm. No foul.

"What...?" Nemesys sizzled in surprise, barely opening his jaw to emit a sound. He'd never experienced such a brash move by a dog, much less a puny, lame mongrel like this. The indignity of this slight sent a visible shiver down his spine, while the crowd of hungry onlookers gasped at this obvious breach of protocol.

Feeling that the dog's muzzled, unintelligible reaction was a good sign that his thoroughly unplanned shock and awe strategy was working, Rat Dog sensed that he had gained the upper hand. He turned to face Nemesys and gave him a dose of what he knew best: to howl invectives.

"What in the name of dog's kingdom are you?" he inquired.

Nemesys remained too befuddled to utter a word, yet he instinctively yawned to display his large, shiny fangs for all to see.

"Ouch!" Rat Dog opined, twisting his head to and fro. "It appears you've got major tartar buildup there. Seems the big guy has been gorging to excess on starches and sugars. Have you seen the teeth fixer lately or considered modifying your diet? It also appears you've been gaining a bit too much tread on the sidewalls since those bloat bags hanging from your ribs don't properly adhere to your frail chassis."

At this point, Blister had made the giant leap to reorient his consciousness from what hadn't yet appeared at the dorco door. He focused

DAISY THE DUMPSTER DOG - A SORDID TALE OF DYSTOPIAN HUBRIS AND CONVENIENT CANINE RATIONALIZATIONS

on the four-legged twerp lodged between his boss and the door, then stood erect and ready to pounce. "Nemesys," Blister belched, "he's a new guy. Doesn't get the rules. Can I kick his hairy behind straight to the moon?"

Rat Dog didn't flinch. His head moved slightly at Blister's comment, but he knew who was in charge and thought it best to go directly for the big kahuna. Besides, he was just getting started with his 'charm and disarm' broadside.

"Uh. Yeah. You still haven't answered my first question. Perhaps you're a bit slow. Much less, you forgot to say 'thanks' for that free bit of dental advice. I'll restate, in case your apparent superpowers aren't exactly in the language of our kind. Here we go for a second try, though my effort may turn out to be fruitless: It's a simple question, big guy. What kind of odd hound are you? I'd say in a pinch that you're a German Shepherd. Yeah, I've met a few in my day. So you're German. Maybe. Shepherd. Possibly. Actually, most of us are aware that it's a sign of insecurity to attach two names to a breed. It's as if you're not certain that others can immediately tell what kind of shepherd you are, so you're forced to append an additional word in front of it. It reeks of obvious and no doubt humiliating insecurities. I suppose it's one of many weaknesses resulting from successive inbreeding. You shouldn't feel bad, though. It can happen to the best of us."

Not taking his keen eyes off the dorco door, Nemesys finally had come to his senses as well. "Hey, pudge boy. You may be new here, and you apparently don't understand the process. You aren't part of The Caste, twerpo. Not even close and clearly not purebred like us. Judging by your mingled, mangled looks, you're below the bottom rung in our society. You'd better get with the game, or your little butt is toast. Literally toast. I'll have you know that I'm chained-up both in spirit and in fact with the Swatter Bowl Mangi. Nobody messes with them, so nobody messes with me. Now, get out of my face and back to your place, which is last in line."

He then peered sideways to frown commandingly at his number two. "Blister, I command you to crunch this swollen tick within your massive jaws and transport the squirming parasite to the back of the queue. It's fine with me if you draw blood, as ticks tend to bleed when they're extracted from the host."

Turning to the large crowd of onlookers, Nemesys continued by joking: "Then we can all observe his frail, piddling legs wriggling helplessly, similar to what his smaller, blood-engorged, brown cousins do when forcibly removed from our hides."

"Gladly, boss," Blister replied, taking a crouched step towards Rat Dog.

"Wait there a moment, Big Guy," Rat Dog warned, holding his one good front paw up. At that, he rolled over on his side because his broken leg couldn't maintain his excessive body weight.

Every dog in the dorco area, except for Rat Dog, his pals, and Nemesys, broke out in laughter.

Unintended but undaunted, Rat Dog slowly perched himself upward, his three good legs shaking, and resumed as if nothing had happened. "I say, you still haven't answered my one, simple question. Not that you're intellectually capable of doing so. Here it is again, and I'll say it slower this time. Do you know what you are? I offered German Shepherd, but that's apparently too elevated on the status perch for you. Perhaps you're one of those disgusting mongrels that, through some ill-fated genetic mishap, turns out looking German Shepherd-ish, though you're probably the farthest thing from that superior breed. Do I have those facts about right?" Rat Dog raised his eyebrows in question, appearing as if he was truly curious.

"Don't you dare call me a German Shepherd again!" Nemesys warned angrily, shifting his eyes momentarily from the dorco door to view the mongrel still quaking with bodily fear before him. "I'm Malinois. Belgian Malinois, the truest of breeds. Smartest of breeds. Every-

DAISY THE DUMPSTER DOG - A SORDID TALE OF DYSTOPIAN HUBRIS AND CONVENIENT CANINE RATIONALIZATIONS

one here seems to get that but you, little bloodsucker. You, who understands nothing of The Caste and your lowliest place in it, if at all."

But Rat Dog, unhindered by the fear coursing through his veins, persisted. "You're mumbling Gobbledygook, buddy. Like everyone else here, I could give a rip about your insignificant caste thing that you cling to so tightly like it's a pee-soaked blankie in your flea-laden doggie bed. Regarding the Malinois bit, I think not and don't know who might have sold you that bill of goods. You apparently bought into the narrative, however, which makes sense given your obvious insecurities. I've seen real Malinois before and even been to Belgium in my travels. You can't possibly be Malinois as they are far more alert, stately, and muscular than you. I could add a few more adjectives there, but you're no Belgian and clearly no Malinois."

Rat Dog paused to take a breath and see if any of this was making sense to the onlookers. "I'm pretty expert at this kind of assessment, and I'd guess you're a Shepherd half-breed, at best, and another non-canine mixture. Chinchilla, perhaps? Lots of those hot messes these days with all the genetic manipulation and off-target mishaps. Yep, mishap could explain you. But I suppose you've adroitly been pursuing that purebred narrative for a while and have sold that story to unsuspecting doltish types. More power to you, if so. One of my favorite sayings is 'Repetition Breeds Belief,' and you're a shining example of that. Perhaps your friends will continue to believe what you say, assuming you have any real friends, of course."

That last line hit a particularly sensitive note. Nemesys was always worried about his position atop the local hierarchy; constantly fighting to stay on top. He was never certain where he stood and whether his friends were just that or only hangers-on, grifters, or groupies who followed him obligingly so they could get second or third dibs on Delights. Then again, maybe they were overt ladder climbers, wanting to shoulder-rub with the hoity-toity he regularly chummed with in The Caste. It all bugged the hell out of him.

Even before Rat Dog had taken his first step toward the dumpsters, his newly found friends sensed the rest of the day was not going to go well, and they were right. Things were hard enough as they were. Finding sources of clean water to drink. Avoiding the fast boxes on wheels. Empty belly 'skip days' of no Delights. Storms and freezes. Unruly cats. Coyotes. Nobody wanted to look for trouble, as it was plentiful to find. Nobody but Rat Dog, that was. Yet they knew one thing. This good-for-nothing, persistently annoying, impudent mutt could be occasionally entertaining, as they had just witnessed. He might be a good addition to the team, assuming he could keep his mouth in line.

Throughout the troublesome exchange, which was primarily Rat Dog's disparaging monologue, their canine instincts had begun kicking in. Big dog versus little dog. Big dog gang versus little dog alone. Helpless, tubby runt with a cast.

They'd seen dogfights before, even had been in a few, and none wanted that to occur. And the local packs looking on, mostly their friends, were not about to join their side in the forthcoming fray, should one occur. The three knew that Rat Dog, considering his miserably indefensible physical state, would be unable to talk or walk his way out of the mess he had dug himself into. Someone or multiple ones had to leap into the inevitable.

EPISODE 319 – DELIGHTS

BLISTER WAS STILL CHOMPING at the bit, waiting for Nemesys to give the 'attack' nod that he sensed was about to arrive.

'The gall of this newcomer to say such things to the Exalted One!' he considered. 'No dog goes up against Nemesys. He's got the pedigree. He mingles with the highest status creatures who rub their backs in the rarefied air of the most high Mangi and all that they control and stand for in society. Such status is not easy to come by and requires lots of stinky favors. Unpleasant sniffing of butts and doing the deeds mandated by the canines in The Caste, whoever they might be.'

In reality, Blister had never experienced a close encounter with members of The Caste, beyond Nemesys, if he even was a member. Certainly, the Swatter Bowl Mangi were included in that group. He once saw two of them from a distance after Nemesys pointed them out, their distinctive black neck cones being hard to miss. But the others? He knew they must exist somewhere else.

The Caste and their enablers pulled the levers in society, though the Swatter Bowl Mangi among them stood at the top of the pile. They barked out rules and edicts, made decisions, and interpreted ancient concepts from the long dead but transcendently revered canines known as the Demidogs. Yet, none of these lofty dances of dominance and decisions were anywhere close to Blister's own lowly bailiwick written in his destiny from birth and bloodlines.

Blister was the muscle. That was his purpose in life, and he had to look the walk, look the look, walk the walk, and walk the look, as he considered it his only strong point. If he could only slay dragons with words like the stupidly courageous but helplessly pathetic black-eyed rat sitting in front of him, then he could match his physical prowess with a wicked, talented tongue and forethought, planning, and cunning to boot. If he had that, he'd surely be elevated a few rungs on the dominance ladder.

However, he wasn't capable of such. He understood that he'd always be relegated to playing second fiddle to Nemesys, the real boss in the area. But somewhere, deep in the recesses of his thick skull, he wished he could be free from the burden of always serving that master, or any canine master, for that matter.

Nemesys, on the other hand, fully understood that he had an image to constantly uphold. Firstly, there was his gang of six who regularly trailed him and did his bidding. One of those biddings was to engage in physical confrontation, though that was always the last resort to canine interchanges. In fact, he couldn't recall the last time that he himself had jumped into a dogfight. It had been many moon passes because Blister substituted for him in recent times. Secondly, the entire community accepted his regal state, and most were present and observing as these regrettably vocal events unfolded. Nobody except the Swatter Bowl Mangi or certain Caste members had the wherewithal to dress him down in the manner that the vile little worm just did.

So, he couldn't pretend it didn't happen and prance along his merry way. Besides, it appeared at this point that the Delights might not be forthcoming, and none of the dogs in the crowd would be jolly about that. On a good day, Delights would take first priority over all things, and he might take care of the mealy-mouthed maggot later. But not today.

Having dug himself deeply into this regrettable hole, Rat Dog's eyes were bulging fiercely out from his tiny forehead, and his whole body continued trembling uncontrollably. He was tapping out on invectives and hoped that a few might magically surface from his spent mind. If he could only create a bit more delay with further verbal slights, it might allow a window for the dorco door to open, after which the vitriol he unleashed would soon be forgotten.

But it was not in the cards, as Nemesys was finally ready to take action. He gave Blister the nod to proceed.

Sensing his utter helplessness and potential bodily demise in the moment, Rat Dog did what any sensible, defenseless canine would do: he rolled again on his back, purposely this time, to expose both his soft, blubber-rich underbelly and his cast. Three of his four legs were bent limply in full surrender. He also hoped that the visible amplification of the cast would create sufficient sympathy from his attackers and the crowd in general to forestall bloodshed. Specifically implying his own bloodshed.

Having been given the nod, however, Blister had already begun to pounce, but he stopped short after observing Rat Dog's pathetic rollover. Hovering above the incapacitated blob, he stared momentarily at Nemesys. "He's waving the universal surrender white flag," Blister complained. "How do you suggest I get a bite on him?"

Nemesys was not happy at this disruption in what should have been a clean and easy 'lift and throw' procedure by Blister. "I suggest you grab him by his tiny back legs flailing in the air there, then toss this engorged tick mouth over the hedge, assuming you're dog enough to execute the job!"

At his command, Blister lunged toward Rat Dog's legs to do just that.

Then all hell broke loose.

EPISODE 320 – SUCKERS

DURING THE VERBAL EXCHANGE, Daisy, BadBoy, and Dug had been slowly approaching Nemesys and his compadres. Luckily, nobody had yet noticed their breach of lineup protocol. The crowd had shifted their eyes and hopes away from the dorco door, and all were watching the entertaining but disturbing proceedings in front of them. As of late, few had seen a good dogfight, and most simply wanted to sit back and wait to see what might happen.

Right as Blister opened his mouth, BadBoy jumped forward to place himself between Blister and the upturned tick. Catching an unanticipated mouthful of matted brown hair, Blister immediately backed off in surprise.

"What's this?" he coughed, choking on a clump of the soiled stuff.

The surprise intervention gave BadBoy an opportunity to use his snout to roll Rat Dog to his side and grasp him by the fatty skin on the back of his neck.

"Ouch, you careless beast!" Rat Dog wailed. "That's my neck you're biting."

BadBoy turned and bolted toward the nearest hedgerow, while Daisy and Dug sat there, stupefied. They realized that, in their haste to save their new friend, assuming they wanted to consider him as that, they had no plan once they got up to the stage. And stage it was. BadBoy was rapidly striding toward the hedge, with Blister and a few of Nemesys' crew in hot pursuit. Daisy and Dug were at that line, the line you don't cross, between Nemesys and the dorco door.

DAISY THE DUMPSTER DOG - A SORDID TALE OF DYSTOPIAN HUBRIS AND CONVENIENT CANINE RATIONALIZATIONS

Daisy sniffed the air momentarily, though this sniff was not her usual 'you don't matter, so I'm sniffing the air' sniff. It was the lingering stench of Rat Dog's sweaty body. She'd never smelled that before. Since so little of her brain was actively focused on the danger at hand, she stood innocently at attention, overwhelmed and excited by the smells that were emanating from the entire crowd, given the possibility of a large conflagration.

Dug wasn't concerned about sniffing anything, however. She was assessing the likelihood of making it out alive, or at least relatively untouched. "Back off!" she warned, as Nemesys and his residual three thugs approached them. "We aren't looking for trouble; only for fairness."

Nemesys stopped in his tracks and signaled his troupe to halt as well. "Fairness? Fairness? You brought that rat into our nice, controlled enclave, then tried to protect him after he insulted me? Insulted all of us?"

Nemesys was particularly pleased to use that last line, since he had heard rumblings about always thinking of himself first, and he felt he needed to be a bit more inclusive. "There are rules here, rules established long ago about how our society behaves. About everyone's proper place. That's what matters. Fairness matters not in these parts, only the rules as defined and interpreted by the Swatter Bowl Mangi. You should know that by now."

In her anxiety to elicit a sensible retort, Dug was slobbering profusely and hardly able to yap properly. "Look, buddy, we just met the dude. He's harmless. Big mouth with little else of value. He hasn't been given the chance to acclimate to these new surroundings. Besides, he recently made a heroic jump and apparently damaged both his leg and personality. Nobody gains by further injuring an already injured canine. It simply looks bad on the surface, right?"

While Nemesys and gang moved slowly toward them, Dug and Daisy instinctively were tracing backward, very close to the dorco door.

Dug was so engaged licking slobber from her mouth and nose that she was running out of mental bandwidth to murmur anything else that might make sense.

It was one of those moments when the worst could have happened. Or not. Dug? Slobbering. Daisy? Nose in the air. Nemesys and gang? Teeth bared and ready to rumble.

"Speak!" Dug whispered to Daisy. "I need some help."

But it wasn't Dug's whisper that did the trick. It was a sound.

"Did you hear that?" Daisy asked.

"Hear what?" Nemesys replied angrily, crouching his front legs to take the first pounce at fresh dog meat.

"The door," she replied.

"The door what?" Dug managed to blurt out. She wasn't quite catching what Daisy was up to. In fact, Daisy wasn't quite sure, either.

"The door. I hear something," she cautioned. "Look, I may be a hybrid, but I've got the best set of ears around here, and I hear interesting goings on behind the door. Creaking and shifting and maybe standies walking in the distance. Seems like it's getting closer, too."

At this suggestion, Nemesys and his crew, all who had emulated their boss in the 'crouch and pounce' position, relaxed a bit and stood up straight, ears as erect as possible. "I hear nothing, oh wimpy white wizard of ears," Nemesys snarled. "Nothing but a distraction. Do you take me for a witless wimp? A mixed mongrel? I've got ears, and I hear not a peep."

"Wait!" she countered. "Do you smell that? I could swear it's foul. Chicken, perhaps. Cooked meat, certainly. A sweet hollandaise sauce, me thinks. And fruit? Cooked apples? Pears? It's sugary, starchy stuff. Not my cup of tea, personally, such sweets, but somebody might like it. If I was a betting girl, I'd say they're up to something quite enticing behind the doors."

Both Daisy and Dug noticed that their wanna-be attackers had become totally preoccupied with the thought of potential Delights. Sali-

DAISY THE DUMPSTER DOG - A SORDID TALE OF DYSTOPIAN HUBRIS AND CONVENIENT CANINE RATIONALIZATIONS

va was dripping from their snouts, a sure sign that this was the moment to skedaddle.

The two discreetly tiptoed backward and joined the would-be attackers as they intently stared at the dorco door. In fact, all packs in the vicinity had breached normal protocol by this time, first anticipating a fight and now expecting delicious Delights. Doing their best to shimmy their butts imperceptibly to the rear, Daisy and Dug carefully wiggled to the outer ring of canines without being noticed. Once in the clear, they bolted as fast as they could, away from the dorco area and toward the comforting and confusing maze of hedges.

So relieved that they had not been maimed or killed in a fracas, Dug couldn't help herself. "Suckers!" she howled, a distance away.

Nemesys was so focused on Daisy's descriptions of forthcoming Delights that confusion reigned supreme in his entitled mind. Go, or stay? Chase, or eat? "Get them," he barked at his remaining three lackeys, and off they ran. But Daisy and Dug had such a significant lead, and they knew their way so well around the underbrush of the hedges, that Nemesys' gang never caught them.

After the crowd dispersed, Nemesys continued his vigil adjacent to the dorco door. He wasn't about to be one-upped by a donkey-eared, half-breed mutt. When the magical cuisine finally arrived, he knew he'd get to eat it all, just as she described. All the Delights. To his misfortune, he rested there for the night on an empty, angry stomach.

EPISODE 321 – DINGO

"KNOCK, KNOCK. AM I disturbing anyone's sweet slumber?" Dingo croaked in his high-pitched voice. He was back after an extended visit with a good friend. "I understand there was a bit of harrowing action here yesterday."

His head was sticking through the hedge opening into their lair. But after the previous day's events, not everyone was in the mood to joyously arise.

"Dingo!" Daisy shouted. "Dingo, you're back! Mega nice to have you here. Did you enjoy your visit?"

Upon Dingo's arrival, Daisy began her usual bouncing up and down in their lair, causing a general ruckus. She normally did this activity outside because jumping in the lair caused brush and dust to stir in a very small place for the four dogs. And the fifth was standing outside.

"Who is so rudely disturbing my slumber?" Rat Dog groaned. "If it's that Nemesys creep, tell him I'll gladly meet the wimp outside for his comeuppance. You'd think he'd have had his fill of defeat by now."

"Shut it!" Dug demanded, stretching her short, pudgy body in the small corner where she slept. "As you can tell, Dingo, we have a new visitor, and let's hope it stays that way. A temporary and troublesome transient."

BadBoy refused to wiggle an ear in acknowledgment at Dingo's arrival. He could hardly arouse any form of consciousness after the events of the prior evening. The back of his neck was on fire from carrying Rat Dog for what seemed to be miles before Blister called off the pursuit. Worse yet, Rat Dog persistently nipped at BadBoy's ears and cheeks

DAISY THE DUMPSTER DOG - A SORDID TALE OF DYSTOPIAN HUBRIS AND CONVENIENT CANINE RATIONALIZATIONS

along the exhausting chase, demanding that he must be dropped onto the ground in order to fight mano a mano with Blister and his buddies. BadBoy considered dropping him, but he was in no mood to watch the nasty tick explode in a burst of blood.

"What are you?" Rat Dog expelled in his typical unsociable and utterly inappropriate greeting.

"Say what?" Dingo replied, taken aback by the sniveling chub that could hardly raise his head to greet the new arrival at the lair.

Rat Dog continued to feign little more than casual notice and was extremely unpleased at this interruption. He wanted to sleep. Delights had not come. His entire body was in pain due to being carried in BadBoy's stinky mouth. He didn't get to fight Blister and prove his superiority. Lots went wrong the previous day, and he just wanted to sleep it off and position himself strategically to ensure he could have a shot at first dibs when the afternoon's Delights were scheduled to arrive.

"Are you unintelligent, or unintelligible, or do you even understand the difference?" he whined.

"What in the name of doggie dung do we have here?" Dingo inquired, staring incredulously at Daisy.

"He gimped our way yesterday from nowheresville," she replied, still overjoyed at Dingo's arrival. She sniffed at his feet and put her nose in the air. "You've been places, haven't you?"

"Stories to tell, my loveliest of daisies; stories to tell. But let's get back to the newbie. What gives?"

Rat Dog was again concerned that this new arrival, though obviously not new to the others, might displace his position in what was now a comfortable dirt bed he'd made for himself in the lair. And he was having none of it. "Then I'm sure the places you've visited would be glad to have you back. So why don't you turn your pathetic butt around and shoosh out of here? A few of us are attempting to sleep, and mature canines have the common sense and consideration to let sleeping dogs lie. Can't you see me in here? I'm lying down and don't intend on getting up. I also don't want to engage in petty conversation like you cretins or hear what you have to say about your travels to wherever that might have enticed your witless intellect. Consider it this way, bub. None of this disturbance of yours excites me, and that's all that matters."

At that comment, Dingo decided he'd heard enough. He entered through the doorway to step lightly on Rat Dog's tail and indicate that his rant was about to end.

By now, Rat Dog was gaining back conscious awareness of where he was, how he got there, and the lowly position he undoubtedly held in everyone's eyes after the previous afternoon's brouhaha. All were aware of his utter failure except this new guy, and he thought if he could only put him in his place, it might be a good start. Moving quickly up the dominance ladder was not his particular forte, he knew, but each path had a beginning. "Hey," he sniveled, "scoot your butt off my tail, or you'll get what's coming to you!"

"Apologies," Dingo began. "And you are...?"

"Rat Dog," Dug chimed in, "and he is truly part rat. Possibly full rat, as much as you are an advanced dogbot, amigo."

"Dogbot?" Rat Dog laughed. "Dogbot? I don't know dogbots, but I do know Basenjis. Nondescript canines. Dingy brown on white, or white on brown. But who really cares? They have ho-hum, boring, disinterested markings. Expressionless. A non-functional tail that's ridiculously curled as if mimicking a coiled snake. Forward-standing and off-balance, as if you'd fall on your face at the next slight breeze. Please, can you bark for me, perhaps a quick loud one? That'll tell me if I'm on the right track."

"I'm not sure your peanut can comprehend what a dogbot is, newcomer," Dingo politely replied.

"First," he countered, "I'm no newcomer and suggest that you are actually the outsider at this juncture. Please, though, give a little bark for my amusement."

DAISY THE DUMPSTER DOG - A SORDID TALE OF DYSTOPIAN HUBRIS AND CONVENIENT CANINE RATIONALIZATIONS

Dingo proceeded to bark his mechanical equivalent. But having been put on the spot to perform, he could only evoke a brief, whimpering squeak.

"Pathetic. Simply pathetic," Rat Dog exhorted. "As I indicated, you're a Basenji, or at least a Basenji mix, which implies you are both unsightly and unfortunate. They bark exactly like that, meaning not at all. Please, please, do us a favor and don't try to make that sound in our presence again. It's not worthy of our listening, not worthy of our attention, and really disrespects the entire canine species when you fail at such a half-hearted attempt at being a real dog."

Dingo was perplexed. "Daisy, what kind of vermin did you pick up yesterday? How did this miscreant wander freely into camp? May the watering rains save us if someone invited him here. And the cast on his leg, is this the reason he's uber acrimonious? He's scared he can't defend himself by any other means?"

Before Daisy could respond, Rat Dog interjected, "Oh, buddy. I can defend myself perfectly fine. Come on over here and let me sink these sharp fangs into your disturbing, metallic hide there. Hey, seriously, what the heck are you, anyway? I've never seen a dog made from metal. Were you born that way, dingbot?"

Daisy finally got a word in edgewise. "You heard Dug mention that Dingo is a dogbot, not a dingbot. Dog and robot. That's what he is, and we love him. Best friends!" She began pogo-bouncing again and dislodged a few branches coiled above them.

"Calm down, girl!" Dingo pleaded.

"Yeah," Dug seconded, "you're stirring up tons of garbage in here again. Coupled with BadBoy's incessant shedding, I'm in a constant wheeze state. Please do your hopscotching outside and get the yah-yahs out of your system."

Daisy stopped and stared at Dingo, smiling the best smile she could. "He's a new addition to the pack. Granted, the runt's got quite a mouth, and that mouth already embroiled us in major trouble with the Nemesys cult yesterday."

Dingo's head turned to the side. "What kind of trouble did this pudge boy cause?"

As they updated him about the disturbances of the previous day, Rat Dog was growing increasingly bothered by Dingo's mere unanswered presence. He was going to burst if he didn't speak, so he just let it go. "What gives with you whiny whippets? Why doesn't a single dog in this place possess anything close to my intellect? Am I the only one who's wondering why we're talking to this disgusting contraption standing before us? Yes, the thing that rudely awoke me this morning? Isn't anyone as curious as me as to what makes this apparition run? How is it talking? Why does it look and bark, or not bark, like a Basenji? Why can't I smell it? Why do I hear disturbing gearing and meshing and unnatural noises from its body? Am I dreaming here? Is this a purgatory to which I've been assigned for the crime of being an exemplary canine? Why is nobody listening to me?"

Dug responded, tiring of his bellowing. "Because you're always talking? Because you're constantly rude, biting, and angry? Because you might have caused us to lose the exalted but lowest Caste status that took us so long to obtain? Because you think solely of yourself and your needs?"

"Whoa!" Rat Dog exclaimed, finally rising enough to sit on his haunches. "What intestinal worm has gotten into your goad, big girl? I'm simply asking questions that a half-sentient observer should ask. This Dingobat is something 'para,' as in parasite, and 'normal' that is far from normal. Paranormal. Get it?"

"Settle down," Daisy commanded. As effervescently ecstatic as she was naturally, she, too, was tiring of his baneful bleats. "Again, our longtime friend Dingo is a dogbot. His standie creators intentionally designed him to look and act as if he was a real Basenji. Nothing wrong with that. Any more questions, or can you finally give it a rest?"

DAISY THE DUMPSTER DOG - A SORDID TALE OF DYSTOPIAN HUBRIS AND CONVENIENT CANINE RATIONALIZATIONS

"A rest? Seriously? What's with these disgusting 'dee' names? Who chose those?" he sneered.

They looked at each other, not knowing what he was talking about, yet he continued. "Did you three conspire together in order to thoroughly confuse intelligent canines such as myself? And what was the conversation like when you first met? 'Daisy, meet Dingo. Dingo? Daisy. Dingo, meet Dug. Dug? Dingo. Dug, meet Daisy. Daisy? Dug? The mere thought of that discussion is making me ravenous for water. I'm hydrophilic, not hydrophobic. Although there's one shining light here, and that's Bad Boy. It's probably the only light he's got, but at least his name doesn't start with 'duh', like Duh-ingo, Duh-aisy, Duh-ugh. Definitely dumb! I'm too young for this nonsense."

It was early. Rat Dog hadn't yet taken a drink of water. His breath smelled terribly dead-fishy, far worse than his typically odorous dead-fishy, and he was gagging on it. Assuming that his remarks had established a well-fought, dominant position, he finally relented and relaxed his front legs, carefully setting himself into as comfortable a sitting position as he could muster, given his cast.

"Thank you!" BadBoy exhorted, barely opening his eyes. "I couldn't determine if I had eaten rancid food and was having hallucinations again, or if it was just this chubby tick doing his lip-flapping jive. Given my usual rotten luck, it was the tick, though I'd have much preferred the rancid meal."

Rat Dog nearly responded to this slight, but Daisy's fervent glance indicated that he should clearly back off.

Dingo remained curious. "Let me get this straight. This inconsequential mutt here, the one with the foul mouth, had the cajones to walk straight up, past Nemesys, then sit his butt down between the top dog and the Sacred Door of Delights?"

Dug wasn't about to give Rat Dog credit, saying, "Though it might give the appearance of courage, there's a very, very thin line between courage and stupidity brought about by anger and hunger, as was the case in this instance."

An advanced robotic dog, Dingo's makers provided him with none of the emotions that would endear him to standies. Fear. Malice. Courage. Anger. Joy. He simply didn't possess these, and that made him joyous most times, as happy and go-lucky as a purely logical and stoic dog could be. It was this lack of emotions that ultimately did him in, however, as his one and only standies family could tolerate his dispassionate ways no longer. They threw him out on the front porch for good and closed the door. After wandering endlessly, he came upon this small pack of eccentric canines whom he enjoyed as much as he possibly could, within his program constraints.

"I've often thought about the unfairness of it all," Dingo observed.

"Of what?" Daisy inquired.

"The situation we've discussed on occasion. This unfairness doctrine with the Demidogs and Canistution. How the Swatter Bowl Mangi claim that they're magical and mystical interpreters, and how their interpretations end up advantaging those amorphous, advantageous adherents who are already over-advantaged. Similarly, indulging the indulgent indolents who are already over-indulged."

"Uh. Wait," Rat Dog interjected. "Are you talking about the Canistution? The Demidogs again?"

Dingo pawed pensively at the ground. "It's an idea I've been kicking around and gigaflopping in my flash that could challenge the lopsided status quo."

"Oh, no," BadBoy requested, barely lifting his head to speak. "We were finally quieting the rat down. Please, don't get him started. This one's a literal gagmagnet for others' misfortunes. Look to your left, and he's causing trouble on your right. Turn to your right, and your left is aflame. Don't give him ideas, Dingo, or we'll be booted from here by Nemesys and his duplicitous delinquents."

DAISY THE DUMPSTER DOG - A SORDID TALE OF DYSTOPIAN HUBRIS AND CONVENIENT CANINE RATIONALIZATIONS

"Get me started?" Rat Dog spat back. "I'm not starting anything. I'm just listening to my new friend Dingo to see what he has to say about the status quo, whatever that is."

"There are things you know, kids, and things I know, and things none of us knows for sure but have a pretty clear sense about," Dingo observed. "Mind if I take a minute to educate this unsightly roll of vociferous flesh about what I've come to understand, amigos?"

"Fine with me," Dug confirmed.

"And me," Daisy added.

They peered at BadBoy, who was back asleep.

"And me," Rat Dog thirded.

Dingo raised his front paw and pointed it directly at Rat Dog's tiny, black, runny nose. "I'm warning you not to interrupt with your typical tripe. I get that you enjoy hearing your own poisonous opinions, but you need to take the hint that nobody cares about them. Not until you start making sense, and not until you pull back on the bombast."

For once, Rat Dog said nothing when spoken to. He'd known too many instances where he had snapped replies at comments and things ended badly. Besides, this new guy might have useful information, even an idea to improve his access to the one thing he couldn't shake from his mind, not in his elevated state of craving: the fabled dumpster Delights.

EPISODE 322 – FIDOISH

DINGO TOOK A SEAT and glanced backwards to ensure that no canines were within earshot. What he had to say was known by only a small number of dogs in the local packs.

Unfortunately, few cared sufficiently to take notice of what was happening in their society. Most simply accepted each minute as it came, wondering where their next meal might come from, sniffing the air, finding a safe place to sleep, grinding their snout in something smelly in the dirt, or scratching and licking at skin problems. It was only the rare dog that held a desire to go further, to ask questions, to evaluate the surroundings and understand the implications.

For many, life was one event followed by another, and they conceded willingly to their helplessness in it all. Complain they might about their lowly positions of status, given the hierarchy of The Caste that continued to be enhanced and codified by the Mangi, they just didn't care sufficiently to make the effort to effect the necessary changes and improve their lot.

Daisy was rabidly chewing at her front left paw like she always did when distracted by smells and sounds, while Dug and Rat Dog listened intently. BadBoy remained asleep, snoring lightly.

"Where to start, I wonder?" Dingo began. "The Caste? Demidogs? The Canistution? The Swatter Bowl Mangi? Then there's the Fidoish club or clique or cadre of conniving clandestine canines. So much to cover about the abysmal state of dogdom. Rat Dog," he warned, "I suggest that you sit up at attention, as this directly applies to you and an interesting idea I'm considering."

DAISY THE DUMPSTER DOG - A SORDID TALE OF DYSTOPIAN HUBRIS AND CONVENIENT CANINE RATIONALIZATIONS

At that, Rat Dog obediently rose from his sitting position, his unbroken front leg trembling slightly from the burden of his bloated bulk.

"Good. I'll begin with the Swatter Bowl Mangi," Dingo said.

Immediately, Rat Dog interjected. "You mean the dudes with the big black cones encircling their necks, correct?"

Dingo raised his eyebrows in warning. "Five words from my mouth and you're already interrupting?"

"I counted eight words, which was enough," Rat Dog retorted, sensing he was pushing it.

Dingo continued. "The Swatter Bowl Mangi were long ago granted lifetime positions to call the shots in dogdom. Yes, they are somewhat akin to the local Mangi, but these Swatter Bowl types swathe and sway at the most elevated levels of dogdom. Ultimately, it is they who bark the final edicts on virtually everything anymore, as well as anything evermore. Now, they didn't always run the show. There were once three exalted dens in our caninical hierarchy, each of which had different roles but otherwise established the rules and similar goings on across their areas of responsibility. Sure, these three groups often dogfought and jousted together, but things generally moved forward, nonetheless. In those days, there was a sense of fairness and balance among canines, whether purebred or mongrel. In fact, even cats and other sentient creatures were considered equals to canines. We all had balanced and equitable access to water, Delights, shelter, and that kind of thing."

Rat Dog couldn't help himself, as he'd been in too many near-miss, life-and-death situations with felines. Heck, he hardly got along with canines as it was, much less those sourpussed mouse chasers. "Cats?" he complained. "You let that word spill from your fish lips as if mentioning them was a good thing? Seriously? Who would ever care to share Delights with such annoying, bad-tempered, milk-slurping ilk? What kind of heady nightmare was that?"

"Hey there, oh non-obedient one," Dingo warned, "ever been bitten by a dogbot? Not pleasant, I'm afraid. I have more horsepower in my jaw than a field of stallions, meaning shut it up!"

"Hum. So much acrimony from you," Rat Dog chided. But his tiny brain was banging and mashing, and it was taking all the mental discipline he could muster to keep from interrupting.

"Where was I, then?" Dingo pondered. "The Swatter Bowl Mangi were established way back in the Canistution because of pretty intolerable unfairness for us non-attached canines, meaning those of us without decent standies families to live with. Things were apparently very bad at that time, a virtual dogarchy, but all of this social turmoil occurred considerable moons ago and well before I was created."

"And how did these canines get to be Swatter Bowl Mangi? I forgot," Daisy added.

"Geez, a lot to cover," he replied. "Well, the Fidoish club or clique or cadre of conniving clandestine canines are responsible for much of what we have today, both at the many local bowls where Mangi rule, and more significantly at the most high, uber-vaulted, and ever-exalted Swatter Bowl."

Dug was not happy at that word. "Fidoish? Isn't that name kind of demeaning to us? I'm aware of no canine worth his salt who wants to be called 'Fido.' I'd rather be called 'Waldo' or 'Worthless Hairy Beast' or simply 'Dog' than 'Fido.'"

"Excuse me," Rat Dog requested, "but the word 'Dog' is a part of my name, so that's not a nice thing to say, Dug, especially considering how pleasant and considerate I've been to you since we first met. But forgetting, for a moment, your onerous slight and the damage it may have done to my personal constitution, who are these Fidoish fiends? Four-legged hairy types, or are they standies?"

"Not standies," Dingo confided. "Look, I don't know everything about them that I should, as I haven't had the need to do further research on them. Therefore, please understand that part of this is second or third-paw dirt. The Fidoish club or clique or cadre of conniving clandestine canines pretty clearly detect, select, elect, and erect which special bowsers get to become a Mangi, but most particularly the Swatter Bowl types. They wile and wangle and wrangle their mysterious ways, spending nights and days grooming and boarding gaggles of future Mangi."

"I was groomed and boarded once," Daisy chimed in.

"I meant a different kind of grooming, Daisy," Dingo assured her. "Though not true of all Mangi in all Bowls, the Fidoish club or clique or cadre of conniving clandestine canines hold enough power to have taken effective control of the lubricating leashes across dogdom. They have been manipulating things so slowly, secretly, and surreptitiously, that they are now the primary reasons why our society so serpentinely serves and sustains dogdom's Caste system in the first place. To conclude, the Swatter Bowl Mangi issue edicts that mostly hang the collars of dominion and dominance over our lowly heads. In reality, however, the masters who hold the leashes of the Swatter Bowl Mangi are logically the real top dogs. And that is them."

Upon hearing this idiocy, Rat Dog became livid. To him, living in this new society was akin to stepping in fresh doggy doo. Dingo's explanation made him whine and pine for his old, abusive standies. At least his life at that time was consistently predictable and predictably consistent. "Then you're telling me that this devious den of Fidoish canines define who gets first dibs at my rightful Delights?"

Dingo frowned the best he could. "That and far more. The Swatter Bowl Mangi interpret the mystical rules of the Demidogs, who are long past dead, then issue edicts about how we must live."

Rat Dog was growing thoroughly confused. "Holy crap. Excusing the expression, Daisy, let's get this tale straight," he chuckled. "First, the Fidoish club or clique or cadre of conniving clandestine canines, as you call them, are exalted members of The Caste, which is apparently a group of dirty dogs who only care to benefit themselves and bereft the rest. These Fidoish types get to detect, select, elect, and erect the Swatter Bowl Mangi, and who knows, many of the other Mangi as well. Second, the Swatter Bowl Mangi establish the final rules for this fungible realm in which we live. Rules such as who gets first dibs or no dibs at Delights. Third, these Swatter Bowl Mangi regularly commune with highly revered, ancient, and pretty dead Demidogs to rationalize their edicts. Do I have this about right?"

Dingo sighed loudly. It was complex, indeed, and he knew the rat was trying to simplify it down to what the peanut in his cranium could comprehend. "Sure," he agreed. "Close enough for your needs."

The little guy quivered. "Then it sounds like the Fidoish club or clique or cadre of conniving clandestine canines needs to suffer the wrath of Rat Dog's infamous and acerbic tongue. Hey, I think I'm finally getting to the core of the problem: It's all about these Fidoish types."

"Oh, not so fast, Snippy," Dug warned.

Dingo was himself having trouble recalling every fragment of what he had picked up in various conversations. Part of the problem was that he never had reason to challenge the status quo of The Caste. When you don't need to eat or have shelter or the delicacies of dogdom, such factors simply matter less. He started tapping his front paw on the ground, hoping it might shake something else loose.

"Okay, I just accessed old memory, and here we go. As I recall, the Fidoish club or clique or cadre of conniving clandestine canines are led by a phantasmagorical, chimerical, and hysterical character named Caociphus."

Rat Dog bared his tiny teeth instinctively and wondered, "So I should have a serious tete-a-tete with this Caociphus, then? Is that what you're suggesting?"

"Not quite still," Dingo replied, continuing to tap the ground, almost nervously. "This Caociphus is presumably supported by another canine or canines with a funny name, one that doesn't roll off the tongue, although I lack that feature."

DAISY THE DUMPSTER DOG - A SORDID TALE OF DYSTOPIAN HUBRIS AND CONVENIENT CANINE RATIONALIZATIONS

"Well, come on!" Rat Dog urged in utter annoyance.

Dingo's eyes rolled around as Rat Dog waited for a burst of brilliance.

"Got it! Got it! It's GogMadDog," Dingo squealed with satisfaction.

"Mad Dog what?" Daisy replied. She had come across a lot of stupid canine names in her days, but this one was a doozy.

"GogMadDog, I believe. Gog. Mad. Dog. Honestly, I'm surprised I recalled that in my core. Took a bit longer but was worth it to cough that one up."

With this new revelation, Rat Dog had grown tired of the string of confusing names and convoluted interconnections, but he wasn't about to let confusion stand between him and Delights, as hunger pangs were driving him to absolute madness. "Okay. To summarize on your perplexing and terribly narrated story, I'll try again and hopefully not regurgitate anything liquid or chunky in the process. GogMadDog controls this Caociphus who hangs tight onto the Fidoish leashes. They effectively select the dead Demidog-communing Swatter Bowl Mangi who establish the rules, including whether I get my fair share of dogdom's Delights?"

Dingo sighed again. "Kind of. Kind of right. First, GogMadDog is more phantasmal than Caociphus. He could be one canine but is rumored to be many multiples. Either way, they shimmy, shift, wag, and lift their legs in dark places while holding their privy paws firmly on dogdom's leash. Caociphus is indeed another dingy character, veiled and mysterious, but presumably real. And who is this Fidoish club or clique or cadre of conniving clandestine canines? Well, they're scattered everywhere, but they totally enjoy the power and leverage they wield over the lowly doggies such as us, feeling magnanimous when they throw us a bone. And yes, they fairly directly choose the Swatter Bowl and many lower bowl Mangi who bark out the set of Caste rules that we must follow. Oh, and I forgot to mention the Canistution."

Rat Dog had heard enough. His eyes rolled back into his head, and he fell to the ground, shaking and shuttering.

"What's with the chubby tick?" BadBoy inquired, finally waking at the commotion in the den.

"I don't know," Daisy observed. "Let's see if he gets over it. You can never tell about the nervous conditions of these rejects from the puppy mills. My guess is that it's DNA related, though I don't quite understand that whole concept. Dug, what's your take?"

Dug's head was shaking, as she was quite amused. "I'm guessing the sesame seed inside that head is overloaded by the stimuli of having to make all those connections of logical illogic. It was too much. If he continues to quake and shake and disturb our living space, I vote we drag him outside and hope that water drops from the sky to shock him out of it."

Feeling guilty that he might have overloaded the pudgy pooch, Dingo nudged Rat Dog with his brown, mechanical nose. "Equal chance that he's faking it, in my opinion. But I agree. Let's give him a minute."

Rat Dog indeed was faking it. He figured that excess attention had been paid to Dingo with his overly extended and arduous story, and it was about time that he got noticed. After a few seconds, he stopped rattling on the ground and rose to shake the dust off, causing the crew, excepting Dingo, to hack.

"Dude!" Dug complained. "You're supposed to do that outside. House rules, pinhead."

Then, for effect, Rat Dog forced out a squirt of stinky bile that had been putrefying in his stomach all morning. "Canistution. Canistution," he repeated, still dripping yellow from his worm lips and acting as if nothing had happened. "What is that?"

"It's how our dogdom social structure began," Dingo added. "A set of rules established long, long ago; well before I was manufactured and before any canine alive can remember. Probably a hundred sets of your

DAISY THE DUMPSTER DOG - A SORDID TALE OF DYSTOPIAN HUBRIS AND CONVENIENT CANINE RATIONALIZATIONS

parents ago, assuming you weren't invented in a tube by some moron. Many moons past. In fact, I'm not sure the moon was even around back then."

"And what does this Canistution have to do with anything?" Rat Dog wondered in all honesty.

Dingo thought for a moment. "From what I can tell, a chunk of it still applies to today's world, but certain parts are way beyond outdated and every dog is afraid to update it because they don't trust each other. Lots of things have happened since its basic rules such as sit, stay, rollover, sleep, and shake were developed. The weather shifted. The standies' dogdom experienced tremendous change as well, though I bear little knowledge of that. There were once lots of them and lots more of us, and we were spread out, to lands far beyond the areas we know about."

"Hey. Basenji bumpkin, you've once again trailed off into an irrelevant philosophical rant," Rat Dog opined. "Do I care what things were like for canine grandparents of mine how many moons ago? No. What do I actually care about? Delights. Delights, Delights, and more Delights. What do I have in my belly right now? No Delights. And you never explained how the Canistution plays into the rubbish and refuse you told me about GogMadDog and the rest. Your story is about as interesting and sensible as watching a pooch chase its tail. Amusing for a moment, then utterly useless."

"Not so useless, little tick," Dingo countered. "The Canistution is a set of guidelines the Mangi use to determine how to deal with dogdom's daily dilemmas. Part and parcel to their process, a few of the specially gifted Swatter Bowl Mangi apparently go into a trancelike state, kicking and scratching and rolling on their backs to commune with the ancient and pretty dead Demidogs. Once that's finished, they bark out edicts for all to follow."

Rat Dog was incredulous. At this juncture, he was considering leaving the lair and his newly found friends. If this was indeed how these canines ran their dogdom, could he tolerate this folly for long? Did cats also use similar inane and arcane rules so incongruent to today's heady situations, such as determining fair and equal access to Delights?

He breathed in heavily, as heavily as his adipose-laden body could, and exhaled a huge sigh. "Okay. Okay. I'll need to digest this a bit, since I have no weighty things otherwise in my gut! You mentioned that you had an idea, big guy; you peculiar paradox on four legs. What's this useless brainchild you're considering?"

After observing this interchange, Dug was miffed that Dingo and Rat Dog had been dominating the conversation. She tried watching Daisy for a while as she bit at her paws and licked her belly, but that dull entertainment faded quickly.

"Dingo, do you remember Old Jack?" Dug interjected.

Dingo stopped for a moment to access his memory. He'd known lots of four-leggers with that name. "Do you mean the one who claimed he had seen the endless waters and floated atop large boxes?"

"Yeah," Dug laughed, "he was the Portuguese water dog that always smelled of overripe cod. Well, he was ancient himself, but he claimed he caught wind of a rumor from another very, very old woofer that a pawful of the Swatter Bowl Mangi were purportedly involved in Ponce Powders and similar concoctions."

"Ponce Powders?" Rat Dog asked. "Sounds edible. What are they, and where do I get them?"

Dug ignored his comment and looked back at Dingo. "What Old Jack said seemed to have a scrap of credibility to it. A few of the decrepit dogs said some of the Swatter Bowl Mangi had been there too long, looked too good, and hadn't aged a day. No gray fur on their snouts, per the puppy rumor mill."

"Hmm. I've heard that gossip, too, though nothing was ever verifiable. If true, such a finding could significantly disrupt our entire society," Dingo speculated. "It's already bad enough that the Swatter Bowl Mangi bark commands from their most high positions, all during their

DAISY THE DUMPSTER DOG - A SORDID TALE OF DYSTOPIAN HUBRIS AND CONVENIENT CANINE RATIONALIZATIONS

very lengthy lifetimes. It is more troublesome, however, if such lifetimes never end."

'Never end?' Rat Dog wondered. 'They'd never die? Not get old? Gain back that vitality of youth?'

Rat Dog had seen lots of days already and would have loved to recover the energy that he had as a pup. He was cute once, and the standies loved him. He could do no wrong, and it was fine to pee everywhere in those early days. But once he got bigger, his standies had issues with him peeing in their big box, particularly on the soft, cloth ground. And it wasn't simply that or the pooping in secret hiding places that they always discovered. He quickly lost his luster of youth and boyish good looks. Gained a lot of poundage. Squandered his spontaneity. Got snippy. Started biting his standies, including the ones who were nice to him.

"And how does this powder work, my friends?" he asked politely, for once.

"Consider that this is all rumor and innuendo. My favorite kinds of facts," Dingo offered. "As I recall, the standies had pills or powders or needle sticks that they used on a few lucky or unlucky dogs. This wizardry could make an old dog new, a frail dog strong, or an idiot dog smart. They were termed 'Ponce Powders,' but no canine in his right mind would believe such a thing existed. I'm guessing more like 'Ponzi Powders' than "Ponce Powders.'"

"What does that mean?" Daisy questioned.

Dingo nodded sadly. "That it's likely a scheme to fake out, to cheat the system, to gain advantage where you shouldn't, to issue orders for all to hear, to control all things for all time. To bark loudly that you're engaged in activities to benefit all canines, but then you make decisions to benefit only yourself, your buddies, and your biases. Such Ponce pills or powders could recast the Swatter Bowl Mangi as living Demidogs in their own right, as if they had been granted special superiority by birthright or breeding and now can maintain their exalted positions in dogdom for ever and ever."

He paused for a moment, letting that comment sink-in to the degree it could, given this lot. "But we shouldn't get too riled up and boisterous, as such rumors were never confirmed. It's not like one of the black-coned Swatter Bowl Mangi came here, barked at our door, and confirmed that this was happening. If that was to occur, holy heck would break loose in the kennel, if you get my drift."

If there was only one positive attribute that Rat Dog possessed, one tiny, beneficial aspect to his being, it was an enduring sense of fairness. Given his lowly status, how could he not retain and hold strong to a belief in the rights of all dogkind to share equally in society and its benefits, such as the yet unforeseen and much anticipated Delights?

"I don't agree with any of this," he ruffed, rising up on his fours. "I don't want a clan of mystical Mangi or GogMadDogs or Nemesys acolytes or cats or similar heathen dictating what I can and can't eat. I don't want them pushing their garbage belief systems down my throat like horse pills wrapped in bacon. I'll gladly tear into their hides, given the chance."

Dug chuckled, causing his mouth to drop more slobber onto his already soaked spot in the lair. "Oh, insignificant one of lesser import than a bean fart, please heed my words. You'll not get the chance to do anything. Not after your pathetic show of bravado yesterday where you forced us to pick up the shattered pieces of your relentlessly mouthy ways. And you probably didn't thank BadBoy for valiantly rescuing your shiny hiney from assured destruction."

"But I beg to differ, Dug" Dingo interrupted. "Our insignificant Rat Dog might be of critical assistance in executing this brainchild of mine."

EPISODE 323 – BRAINCHILD

THE AFTERNOON WAS GETTING on, and four of the five were lying listlessly in their lair. It was sweltering, and the combination of stinky breath and musty coats was becoming too much for them to bear. Rat Dog remained fully awake, however, waiting to hear back from Dingo who finally showed up.

"I brought a friend with me," Dingo announced at the front entrance, "and I need to bring her inside before the roving packs get a nose on this."

"I'm not stopping you," Rat Dog retorted. "Where have you been, big talker? I thought you had a grand plan for my Delights. My stomach remains empty, and my mood is sour. And word of caution: I bite when sour."

"Which is most of the time," Dug groaned.

"A warning to you," Dingo barked, "that my friend is here of her own volition. She understands the risks of being discovered."

A cat slowly sauntered into the crowded lair behind Dingo. A beyond ripe, orange and white tabby. Her right ear had been half chewed off, and her left eyelid drooped down awkwardly. Scars from too many catfights crisscrossed her face, neck, and sides, and most of her body was mottled in red and brown scales and scabs. A small, live lizard wriggled in her mouth.

"Don't you dare say a word!" Dingo advised Rat Dog. "Anyone who leaps at her will suffer my wrath, and she's darn good at fending for herself as well."

Upon her entrance, Dug had already 'taken the position' to leap at her and start the chase, but he backed off at Dingo's warning. BadBoy was barely waking and had been around numerous cats in his day, so this was nothing new, excepting the lizard bit. Daisy was trembling with enthusiasm to meet this new visitor.

Rat Dog was immediately on high alert. This sickly creature was larger than him, and he knew she could callously whip him with a single swipe of her claws. He began uncorking his mouth to belch extreme disapproval, but Dingo stopped him flat out.

"Little tick, you best sit your chubby behind on the ground and listen for a moment," he demanded.

"But...," Rat Dog protested.

"But nothing. You won't yip a word." Dingo motioned for the tabby to sit beside him. "This is my good buddy Crusty. Not that I feel compelled to explain her appearance, but she's a vegetarian. She holds that lizard friend in her mouth as proof of her commitment to the cause and as constant evidence of her compelling self-discipline."

Unable to control himself, Rat Dog burst out laughing. "Crusty? Seriously? Could they not have been more creative than that? It's the first name anyone would think of, considering her detestable skin condition. And she's not eating the lizard? I've eaten hundreds in my day. Snakes, too, and larger reptilian fare like alligators."

Dingo's eyes grew wider. "Stop your babbling," he warned again. "If you weren't critical to this afternoon's Delights plan, I'd boot you out of here right now for acting so rudely to our guest."

That was enough to shift Rat Dog's mind to something closer to his heart. "You said 'Delights?' She's bringing us Delights?"

"No," he replied. "In certain respects, Crusty is bringing the Delights to you, yourself."

"Me?" Rat Dog questioned. "How could an old cat get past Nemesys and his gang to grab me my righteous Delights? Not that I'm against the notion."

DAISY THE DUMPSTER DOG - A SORDID TALE OF DYSTOPIAN HUBRIS AND CONVENIENT CANINE RATIONALIZATIONS

"If you'd shut that vile snapper for a minute, I'll tell you the plan," he yelped, hoping the rat would settle down.

Daisy's nose was high in the air. She had never smelled a cat in close quarters, particularly one with such an abundance of skin problems. "Does Rat Dog die in this scheme?" she questioned. "I'm sniffing an unusual degree of danger and intrigue."

Her comment shut Rat Dog up momentarily. Enjoying Delights first, then getting killed, presumably in that order, was not at the top of his plans for the day.

"I doubt it. I'll be nearby, and Nemesys is no threat to me," Dingo assured her.

Dug was curious. If Rat Dog was gaining unique access to Delights, maybe they all would enjoy them. "Can we simply shut our snouts and let Dingo explain his strategy, even if it does involve this grotesque, sniveling creature?"

"Thanks, Dug, for that colorful slight," Dingo responded. "Okay, here's the scoop. None of us can get access to the trap doors on the dumpsters, correct? Only Nemesys, with the assistance of his dodgy gang, has the special key to unlock the trap door that allows Delights to gush forth. Without that key, it doesn't matter when the dorco door opens and how many Delights bags they pile into the dumpsters, because no dog can jump that high into them without hurting themselves in the process."

"Which is why you brought your friend Crusty?" Daisy surmised.

This was the most astute observation Dingo had ever heard from Daisy, and he was dumbfounded. "Well, yes Daisy. Good job at deduction! Indeed, my friend Crusty will soon become a friend to all of us, and she is quite well-connected. She knows a cat who knows a cat who exposed the secret about how to open the trap door from the inside. Got that? No key required. And since she can easily leap her way into the dumpsters, she'll open the door. Once done, Rat Dog can hide in there until the Delights arrive, and he'll enjoy a belly full of first dibs."

BadBoy had been sleeping, but everyone was making so much noise that he was forced to partially awaken. "Why Rat Dog?" he wondered.

"Because he's the smallest of us and won't get noticed by the standies when they bring Delights. Remember when that old hound somehow found his way into the dumpster? It caused all sorts of ruckus with the standies, right when they were about to pour in Delights. They tried and tried to remove that hound. I still don't know how that event ultimately transpired because they chased us away, but we never saw that poor hound in these parts again."

"What?" Rat Dog asked.

Dingo frowned. "What what?"

Rat Dog was quaking at the thought. "Hound found in dumpster eating Delights, then disappears? Zappo? Dog meat?"

"Don't you see," Dingo replied reassuringly, "we want to hide you in the dumpster because you'll easily be mistaken for inedible junk that they throw in there. Just stay still when you hear them coming, don't squeak or squeal, and in a few seconds you'll be enjoying the freshest of meals to your heart's content."

"But why do this at all?" Dug inquired. "When the Delights arrive and Nemesys discovers Rat Dog in the dumpster eating the first picks, he'll not be a happy pup; more like a hostile hound."

"Exactly!" Dingo agreed. "That's what we want; don't you see? The brilliance of my brainchild is in its ability to accomplish two things of equal benefit. One, Rat Dog gets his fill of Delights and stops griping for a day or so. Imagine a day without his whimpering! That is the definition of dog heaven. Two, we get to challenge the whole darn societal status quo, the unfairness and Caste crapola and bias against us mongrels and whelps farther down the rungs of society."

"Including cats?" Crusty voiced in a sultry purr, juggling the lizard in her jaws all the while.

"Yes, my dear friend. For too long have those in charge severely restricted your access to Delights. They've enacted biased and unfair rules

DAISY THE DUMPSTER DOG - A SORDID TALE OF DYSTOPIAN HUBRIS AND CONVENIENT CANINE RATIONALIZATIONS

and restrictions, very selectively using mystical interpretations from some old dead dogs' ramblings to assuage their guilt. They created a society that works perfectly for them and their buds, but it's flat out sucky for us. If we low status canines are being forced to remain repressed as The Caste and their ilk routinely and unfairly exalt themselves and their comrades, one can only imagine how you and your friends in Felinus dos Gatos feel."

"I hear it's pretty bad there," Daisy commented.

Crusty slinked willfully around, rubbing her back against them, knowing they could not and would not chase her. "We cats are used to the hard life by now, especially since The Caste took control, but that doesn't mean we agree with it," Crusty acknowledged.

A million things were running through Rat Dog's limited mind, and he was far too overwhelmed to capture them well. "I don't get it. Don't understand. This unsightly Crusty cat friend of yours, who I'm totally allergic to, is supposed to unlock the dumpster trap door before Delights arrive. Then I simply stroll inside and hide myself temporarily so the standies don't see me as they drizzle Delights into the dumpster. Once done, I start eating. Then Nemesys and cronies open the trap door. They'll see me inside, enjoying the first dibs to which they are most accustomed, and then I die a wretched and painful death on a partially full belly. Is that your master excellent awesome brainchild plan, Mister Wizard?"

Dingo laughed in his high-pitched, Basenji way. "Yes. But no. You won't die. Probably not. If my strategy proceeds as planned, I'll be there to protect your chubby chowholder from getting torn apart."

Rat Dog's eyes were bulging out at the thought. "You? You? A robotic psychotic that hangs with felines? No offense, but I'm not seeing big dog here. I'm not beholding massive muscles or large teeth. I've not observed any capability you have to take on Nemesys and his gang of monster thugs. So you, by your lonesome self, will fend off his thousands of sycophants and miraculously save me from certain death?

Look, lamebrain, I'm at the top of his doggie doo list after yesterday, and this scheme is unlikely to further endear me to him. Rather than endear, this will only 'end' me to him. End. Get that? As in no more Rat Dog."

"You underestimate what our friend Dingo can do when unchained and unfettered," BadBoy added. "It's my guess that, once Nemesys glimpses Dingo in the midst, then baby, he and his gang will back off quickly."

"Midst? What's a midst in this case?" Rat Dog replied. "Or did you mean 'mist,' as in Dingo will suddenly materialize from a mysterious mist in the middle of this heat, then save the day? Either way, will he be right there at the quick and ready? Will he pull me too late from Blister's teeth or prevent them from piercing this canine coat of perfection? This beautiful canine coat?"

"Don't worry!" Daisy pleaded. "Nobody has ever gone up against Dingo and taken the top position. He's one of a kind, as in undefeated."

Out of sheer fear, Rat Dog had begun instinctively backing against the edge of the hedge and was hidden almost fully beneath it. "Because he's never been in a dogfight, no doubt?"

"Oh, I've been in a few, you mouthy tick," Dingo added, "and Nemesys knows that truth. I'm guessing he'll talk a good story; he'll threaten, but he won't attack."

Given the nominal reassurance but fiercely empty belly, Rat Dog finally agreed to the brainchild. "I'm not afraid of death," he bragged. "I've jumped from ten boxes stacked, soaring all the way down to the hard ground. More courage than all of you combined during your whole lives. And if I should go out today, if I go in this untimely manner, be sure to tell them stories about me and how I worked to save you in a final blaze of glory. About how I showed up one day, a handsome stranger, then befriended you with my generous and gentle ways. About how witty and perceptive I was. Gregarious, in fact, with an amazing intellect. About my superior breeding, my heroic, courageous jump, and

DAISY THE DUMPSTER DOG - A SORDID TALE OF DYSTOPIAN HUBRIS AND CONVENIENT CANINE RATIONALIZATIONS

similar exploits. About how I fought Nemesys while I was severely injured with a massive cast enveloping my body. Be sure to tell them that, including and especially the ladies."

Daisy was paying no attention to his jive. Instead, her ears were at full mast. "Hey guys, I'm sensing activity within the big dorco box. We'd better get started since Nemesys may be showing up."

EPISODE 324 – DUMPSTER

THE INTREPID CREW SAUNTERED nonchalantly toward the largest dumpster, right in front of the dorco door, making sure that no canines would take notice of their clandestine activities. Being a cat, Crusty was forced to maneuver carefully across the hedge's edge to avoid getting spotted by strays who may have decided to show up early for the expected Delights delivery. As planned, she jumped into the dumpster and unlocked the trap door. Two abrasive scratches of her paw upon the door signaled to the crew that things were good-to-go.

"Get in there now!" Dingo commanded, noticing a dog advancing toward them from a distance.

Rat Dog was increasingly hesitant and started yapping nervously. "Maybe it's not worth it for me, did you think of that? Maybe I'm the one taking all the risk, and you guys are instigators and accomplices. If Nemesys or Blister grabs me, I won't get the chance to tell him who the real criminals are here. To explain that I was an unwilling dupe, an innocent bystander who was bamboozled into your lurid game."

The dog was now closing in on their gathering, wondering what the commotion was at the dumpster since Delights usually didn't arrive this early. "Get your chubby chump in there!" Dug ordered. She turned her butt around to face him, then booted him with her short back legs.

Rat Dog yelped loudly as he rolled forward, through the swinging trap door and into the dumpster.

"Stop your whining," Dingo commanded, "or you'll expose our plan." And shut up Rat Dog did after discovering a leftover, partial chicken wing as an appetizer for the treats soon to arrive.

DAISY THE DUMPSTER DOG - A SORDID TALE OF DYSTOPIAN HUBRIS AND CONVENIENT CANINE RATIONALIZATIONS

The dog, a purebred, brown and white Corgi, showed up seconds later. He was one of Nemesys' gang members doing early reconnaissance. "What's happening here, lowbrows, and why are you hanging out by the front dumpster? This area is off-limits until Nemesys gives the signal that it's okay for you lower caste creatures to scrounge for leftovers that we are kind enough to leave for you."

Daisy had seen this Corgi before. She felt he was one of the nicer of Nemesys' gang, but he'd more than likely tattle about what he had found. Noticing that Dingo was having difficulty developing an immediate rationale, she lifted her nose into the air and visibly scanned the area. "I heard purring off in the distance and told my buddies we should check it out. You've seen these infamous ears, right? Easily twice any other dog's size, including your own; no offense intended. I can tell you this. We are not about to go sharing the forthcoming Delights with any felines, that's for sure."

Feeling as if he'd sufficiently scouted the situation, the Corgi backed off. "If you see such disgusting creatures around these dumpsters, Nemesys must be notified immediately. We try to keep this place clean and follow The Caste rules to the letter of the law. No cats and no lower canines. Unless, of course, the Felinus creatures follow up after we're done and asleep. Slim pickings for those unfortunate four-leggers, I'm afraid, but this is how we run things in a just and proper society, right? We each have our place, and the existing power structures ensure that our civil society stays civil and societal, in accordance with the Swatter Bowl Mangi interpretations of the Canistution and the mystically divined wishes of our beloved and long-dead founder Demidogs. Are you catching me, Daisy?"

Daisy was slightly distracted, noticing Rat Dog's nails scraping against the bottom of the dumpster as he foraged for additional treats. She knew it was best to conclude the conversation immediately. "All's clear, then, my friend. My ears must have deceived me, which is rare, but we'll gladly give you the snouts-up signal if we discover felines or undesirable canines roaming the place."

"No creature should be found this close to the dumpsters," he replied. "You should back off and attend to your designated lowly places up there on the ridge. Wait your turn, according to the rules. If Nemesys even saw me this close to the main dumpster, he'd take out a piece of my hide. Imagine what he'd do if he saw you and your lowbrow buddies this close, even if you were hunting cats. Best to back away and wait for the dorco door to open, as usual."

Finally, late afternoon arrived, and the various small packs were lined up in their designated spots. Daisy, BadBoy, and Dug were sitting on the hedge ridge.

"I'm nervous," BadBoy admitted. "Never much took to dog fights nor trouble. Tried to stay away from them. Due to my hair, I resemble a bear and am reluctant to be anywhere close to danger since my date with that swarm of bees. Wasn't doing nothing but walking by. Wrong place. Wrong time. Bad day."

"Indeed, friend," Dug added, "that was a bad week for all of us. Your face exploded to twice its size from the stings. We weren't sure you'd make it."

"Didn't slurp a drop of water or eat for moons," he lamented. "After all I've been through in my destitute dog's life, I run into a beehive. When that water drops from the sky, it pours, I hear, and it hasn't stopped pouring for me since I can remember."

Daisy was ignoring the banter, and she wasn't too worried about Rat Dog, either. Mostly, her mind was on the dorco door and sounds or scents coming from that direction. "Either of you notice where Dingo was off to?" she asked.

DAISY THE DUMPSTER DOG - A SORDID TALE OF DYSTOPIAN HUBRIS AND CONVENIENT CANINE RATIONALIZATIONS

Dug, too, was surprised that Dingo was nowhere in the vicinity. "He was behind us when we left the lair, only a few paces away. Shall I see if he went back inside?"

"Don't bother," Daisy replied. "I can't imagine he'd forget that Rat Dog is actively gnawing and grubbing in that dumpster, or that he'll possibly die horribly in a bloody burst of fur and fat today. But that's not what's on my mind right now. I'm hearing dorco activity and smell Nemesys and gang approaching in the distance."

"Wish I could sniff as good as you," BadBoy complained. "I once could when I got sopping wet and this brown cruddy mud and hair fell off me. That day, my mind opened up to a whole new world of smells, but it faded too quickly."

"And I could never smell that well," Dug observed. "Not built into my breed, given this captivating and at times exacerbating salivating. My types are bred for companionship and fellowship, not smelling smells like you Daisy or smelling bad like you, BadBoy."

"Though my eyes work okay when not covered by hair," BadBoy added, "and I can see Nemesys and Blister and that darn Corgi, as well as his other purebred derelict doggies. Observe how they prance and dance toward their lofty positions!"

And prancing they were. Nemesys was in the lead with his head and nose held high, peering at the various packs in waiting, as if he alone ruled over the entirety of dogdom. Blister followed the requisite distance behind, along with the others. Once at their designated spots, they sat down, stomachs grumbling and on edge since they hadn't eaten anything the previous day.

Though Daisy's petite mind was still engaged in sounds and smells, Dug was taking a second swipe at her comment. "Daisy, you wondered about Dingo's whereabouts?"

"Uh-huh. Quiet, I hear movement behind the door."

Dug raised her eyebrows. "But don't you imagine if Dingo is not around, Rat Dog might actually and truly die trying to fight his way out of the mess he's gonna surely face? Not that I care."

"Mess?" she repeated. "Dingo will show. He's a dogbot. It's not in his system to forget important stuff. Please be quiet, though, as I hear more activity."

"Dug's right, and I'm heading down there," BadBoy observed. "It took all I had yesterday to save that rat's life, and I'm not about to let Nemesys or Blister tear him apart. Saving that witless chub was one of the best, most useless things I've done in my life, and I'd do it again if required. Even for him."

BadBoy stood and slowly ambled down the ridge toward the dumpster. Dug was concerned the old guy would have to fight them alone. "I'm going too. Daisy, are you coming?"

Daisy was utterly preoccupied and perturbed at being interrupted in such concentrated concentration. "Coming? Where?"

"To protect the rat. Didn't you hear a word we were saying? Dingo has disappeared, Delights are about to show up, and Nemesys and cohorts will tear into the annoying boy's hide when he rolls out of the dumpster like a stuck pig. Will you join us in the fight to save the worthless chump?"

For a moment, Daisy was in shock at the mention. She loved everyone, including Nemesys and Blister, and couldn't imagine getting into a tussle with them. It was not in her nature to fight. Talk? Yes. Leap like a frog? Yes. Smell? Yes. Hear? Yes. But fight? No.

"Well," she began, "I'll be glad to accompany you. I can't imagine that bad things will happen, right? There's enough for all, right? These guys won't do dirty deeds to maintain their positions and status in The Caste, right? They'll back off and bark a bit, but not bite. Right? They won't pop him, will they?"

"Not sure," Dug guessed. "This dumpster situation and Dingo's plan are quite alarming, and we appear to be ill-prepared for what's coming next. Where in tarnation is he?"

The two started traipsing the same path that BadBoy took mere seconds before, and he was already within a few uncomfortable paces of where Nemesys stood.

EPISODE 325 – DORCO

THE DORCO DOOR OPENED, finally, and two standies grabbed multiple bags, throwing them into the dumpster closest to the door. It was that same dumpster of the three, the one where Rat Dog was cowering in fear of getting crushed as bags of Delights rained down upon him.

All dogs' eyes were fixated on the dorco standies and the bags. Every head from every canine in every pack was nodding in sync with the movements of the standies. All were enthralled at the grace and form they exhibited as the heavy items were lofted into the three large bins. Hearing the standies laughing as the last bag was thrown, no dog could determine if the laughter was from an inside standie joke or if the standies were simply amused by the dozens of four-legged canines waiting for Delights to be delivered.

Nemesys was intently focused on their activity. His stomach had been growling through the night, a very lonely and cold night, waiting for the standies to show. Thoughts about how the prior day transpired had circulated through his mind in a continuous howl and were so jumbled that he knew only one thing: if a trace of that adipose-laden chihuahua ingrate appeared nearby, he would get what was coming to him.

Striding regally to the trap door, as he always did, Nemesys gave the official nod to his key-bearer, a purebred yellow Lab following meekly in his footsteps. Being the most intelligent in the gang, the lab's only real purpose was to jimmy and jostle the key into the appropriate hole that released the trap door from the outside, thereby allowing Delights to pour forth. Trouble was, he was having trouble.

DAISY THE DUMPSTER DOG - A SORDID TALE OF DYSTOPIAN HUBRIS AND CONVENIENT CANINE RATIONALIZATIONS

"I think a bag must be wedged in the door," he said to a noticeably impatient Nemesys. "It's always worked before. Insert key in jaw, grind it a bit in the hole, then the door flies open, and bags fly out."

Nemesys was growling angrily and appearing more incensed by the moment. It was bad enough that Delights failed to arrive the prior day. Bad enough that the tick got away with demeaning him and mouthing off generally. Bad enough and kind of embarrassing that he'd slept out there and they still didn't arrive. And now, the glorious process of his gang taking first dibs at Delights was delayed by his incompetent yellow Lab. He peered at the crowd, sensing they could be easily aroused to anger if this activity suffered catastrophic failure.

Then they heard a burp. A loud, obnoxious burp, emanating from the dumpster. The obtrusive sound bounced and resounded off the dumpster's steel walls. All was quiet for a moment, then another belch arrived, followed by a sonorous, substantial string of farts.

Nemesys was mystified by the sound. "What the heck is going on in there?" he wondered aloud.

"Sounds like another...," the Lab began.

"Shut up!" he demanded, realizing that if any cat or canine was to gain first dibs before him, the chosen one, he could lose substantial status in the eyes of the packs who were hungrily awaiting their turn at Delights. That would be the worst thing and could cause him to tumble from being number one to just being another lowly dog in the mix. Even given his purebred lineage, his connections in The Caste, his chumming with certain of the Swatter Bowl Mangi, and his occasional hobnobbing with the likes of Caociphus, he understood that dogs at his level were expendable. Local top dog status was never guaranteed and always subject to the whims of The Caste.

With the loudest, meanest growl a Belgian Malinois could muster, he took control of the unruly situation. "Get whatever vermin is in the dumpster out of there immediately!"

At that call, Blister and five hangers-on advanced stealthily toward the trap door.

"Kick it!" Nemesys demanded, staring intently at Blister, and the boxer obliged his master.

"Ouch!" Rat Dog yelped. "Hey there, canine scum. How dare you kick at my door without knocking first!"

And at that, the trap door finally flew open. Rat Dog rolled forward ignobly, sliding outward atop a torn, white garbage bag. He was gloriously covered in barbecue glaze, with a satisfied gaze of serenity and satiation on his face. As further evidence of his unrepentant sin against all things appropriately ordered for the benefit of the few and fortunate, a slice of half-eaten pepperoni pizza was precariously stuck to his right loin.

Though infuriated at the sight, Nemesys tried to stay calm. He knew that if he went fully ballistic and charged angrily to snap the runt's neck, that response might be construed as excessive force. In fact, he couldn't recall the last time a canine actually died in a dog fight, though a few in which he'd been involved in the past had resulted in serious injuries.

In these presciently precious moments, moments of saving face, of maintaining status in The Caste, of complying with and conforming to what he knew were the fluid and ever-changing decisions and derisions of the Swatter Bowl Mangi, he couldn't simply exterminate the overfed perpetrator then hope for the best afterward.

Sure, his allies were the undisputed power brokers, had been for forever it seemed, and might always be during his lifetime. But he couldn't spend all his hard-earned coin with them on this one instance by exacting too high a price from the ill-mannered imp. No, he felt that the damage inflicted should teach a lesson about the high altitudes of

DAISY THE DUMPSTER DOG - A SORDID TALE OF DYSTOPIAN HUBRIS AND CONVENIENT CANINE RATIONALIZATIONS

Caste status and low lowliness of others, but not inculcate a final, fatal lesson that could hound him forever.

So, as many politicians do to avoid taking responsibility themselves, Nemesys assigned the dirty task to a lesser being.

"Blister," he barked ferociously, "seize this miscreant who cares little for our orderly society and the fair, innocuous, and fairly innocuous rules we operate under, and show him what it means to behave properly."

That phrase, 'what it means to behave properly,' rang a few bells for Rat Dog. He'd heard it too often from his standies, usually after he had poopled or puddled or chewed on a standie's paw wear or gnawed on gnawable items they stupidly left around the big box.

He also understood that these might be his last moments. Lying spread-eagle abreast the half-torn bag of Delights, he peered upward at the big expanse and wondered what else might be up there besides birds. He thought of all the things his wonderful mind could have accomplished had he been given a reprieve just this once, a chance to survive this calamitous causal chain, and he felt dogdom would sorely miss his significant contributions. But somehow, the Delights he devoured were entirely worth coming to such an ignominious end.

Blister was hesitant to execute the command as he had never actually killed a dog. Sure, he'd bitten quite a number of them, but those were usually modestly damaging injuries to confirm that Nemesys was the dominant dog and shouldn't be challenged. And it was okay that he did this for his boss.

Besides, according to the Canistution and edicts from the Swatter Bowl Mangi and other caninical ideas and beliefs lost in the ether, he understood that he wasn't the right breed for a higher position in dogdom and never would be. He had to accept that fact and simply execute his master's bidding. Maybe even executing a real, live execution in this case.

Taking a few milliseconds to size-up the bloated tick, he thought it best to avoid the three long-clawed twigs that were wriggling upward. They appeared a bit foreboding, and he didn't feel like breaking teeth on the whitish cast that obscured the fourth twig. If he could nudge the pudge over, he thought, off its back and onto its belly, one clean crunch on the neck might do the job.

"Don't kill him," Nemesys whispered. "I only want him visibly maimed to teach our onlookers a memorable lesson about maintaining their lowly status in the scheme of things."

As Blister nosed the listless Rat Dog onto his belly, he immediately felt the sharp, unpleasant sensation of tiny dog teeth piercing his jowls repeatedly. He'd never experienced such painful sensations in his life.

As this was transpiring, BadBoy had quietly shimmied forward and was within striking distance of Blister. In fact, many of the local pack dogs had moved closer to the activities at the dumpster, and nobody was expecting BadBoy to defend the helpless tick a second time. Both were now ready to pounce: bloody-nosed Blister at Rat Dog, and BadBoy at Blister.

"Eh, eh, eh," a high-pitched voice yipped from behind the dumpster.

"Dingo!" Daisy exclaimed, springing in excitement and fear. "Dingo, Rat Dog's gonna die right now!"

"Not on my watch," Dingo assured her as he stepped carefully toward the canine confrontation. "Blister," he began, appearing completely unruffled at the impending danger, "I suggest you take a second to compose yourself. You don't really want to slay this vile beast, do you? Think of how it would look in your legacy, that future famous and oft-told story of Blister the Boxer that's yet to be shared in boxerdom. So, consider your next move carefully, my friend. How weak might you appear by taking this insignificant one out permanently? He's about the size of your head, buddy, or would be if he lost a bit of poundage. Nobody wants a reputation that they injure smaller, incompetent, or al-

DAISY THE DUMPSTER DOG - A SORDID TALE OF DYSTOPIAN HUBRIS AND CONVENIENT CANINE RATIONALIZATIONS

ready impaired doggies, do they? Even Nemesys should see how pathetic that is."

"Get away from here!" Nemesys warned, backing up as if he was positioning to strike at Dingo.

"Nemmie. Down boy!" Dingo urged. "You're smarter than this, and we can predict how things will end up if you come at me. Not good for you, and not a good look for your own legacy, either, to suffer additional, unnecessary embarrassment in front of this extensive canine crowd. Why don't you let this one go, huh?"

He peered at the crowd, a little unsettled that all eyes were focused on him. "So, Nemmie, consider the facts of the case before executing judgment. New pooch comes to town. Doesn't understand the rules of The Caste. Never heard of the Canistution or Mangi. Only wanted a chance at enjoying first dib Delights. It's not as if the standies chucked the bags right in front of you or otherwise pointed directly at you to have Delights for yourself alone. No, they threw them in the dumpster, which implies fair game and the potential for each here to partake equally. It's just that the rules you tend to tell yourself, your own distorted, constantly repeated narratives, inform you that this ritual process is fair to all. But we know these rules or ways or customs are painfully egregious and onerous to the multitudes among us with lesser status. So, why don't you let it slide for today, then we can get back to our lairs or dens and have a good laugh about what happened?"

"Nemmie?" Nemesys howled in unrestrained anger. "You called me that? Nobody disrespects me in such a way."

"Apparently I do," Dingo countered, smiling the best he could for a dogbot. "But wow! If you're this sensitive when called such a cute name, which is a pretty natural thing for one to do, it might help you to start grooming your sense of self-worth as often as you groom your Malinois coat."

Nemesys was trembling with anger but not making moves to attack. "You'll not get away with this travesty of proper canine nature. I'm taking this to The Caste, and you'll see who's boss when I'm through with you."

Dingo nodded approvingly. "Great; please do that. Of course, if you want to complain, you'll first need to go to the Feeder Bowl Mangi for an evaluation. I don't believe your sway is so strong there. Too bad you have no direct routes to your lords and leash holders among the Swatter Bowl Mangi, at least per the Canistution that they love to hide behind."

Even with his six followers in tow, he knew he'd not likely triumph in an immediate altercation with Dingo, and Nemesys sensibly backed off. "Oh, mechanical monstrosity that can't bark properly, I'll be glad to confront the local Mangi with this preposterous and intentional breach of protocol."

"And I'll be right there with you to argue Rat Dog's case, Nemmie. In fact, I doubt this small disagreement is significant enough to ever warrant attention from your omnipotent Swatter Bowl comrades. Unfortunate for you, buddy, since the lofty connections you hold so close to your hairy chest appear not to have jurisdiction in this matter."

"We'll see about that!" Nemesys woofed hoarsely. "You and your pathetic evil weevils will be sorry you ever crossed me."

Then he signaled to his crew to grab a few unopened bags of Delights and drag them off to their lair. Once they were a good distance away, the remaining canines got dibs at untouched Delights for the first time, and they were quite happy about that.

EPISODE 326 – RESCUE

"DAISY!" BADBOY UTTERED, LIFTING his chin off the ground. "Would you please stop pacing back and forth? It's been a grueling day, and I'm trying to rest before the coming Delights delivery."

Daisy was quivering with anticipation. "I can't see how a single one of you can sleep like a dog on the bed while poor Dingo is at the Feeder Bowl, pleading his heart out on behalf of Rat Dog." She then turned and looked sternly at the disinterested chub. "And you! You didn't have the decency to go there with him. He's doing this for you, tiny troublemaker. But what are you doing? Lying in my spot, of all things, and taking no notice that he's defending your actions."

Rat Dog lifted his head slightly and yawned slowly, as if to amplify his lack of concern. "I got out of it what I needed and could care less what that hapless Basenji faker is doing. You don't seem to get it, Daisy, that only the best of us, the most astute and competent, are able to place our priorities in proper order. Food first. Water second. Sleep third. Shelter fourth. All else pales in comparison and is not worthy of consideration. Now, for once I agree with that unkempt slob over there. Your pacing is interrupting my sleep, which is most disturbing. If you persist, I'll have to take certain steps. Nobody can predict how savage I might become if you don't stop, but probably best for you to heed my warning and clam yourself."

"Clam yourself?" she repeated, still pacing in the lair. "You meant to say that I should calm myself."

"No," he rebutted. "Shows how little you understand of the world or its wisdom. It's effectively a portmanteau, a combination of two words or concepts. Calm yourself is one, and clam your trap shut and let me sleep is the other. 'Clam yourself.' I sympathize with your inability to grasp this simple concept, but even a cat would understand that colloquialism."

With this much conversation occurring during the hot mid-day nap, Dug had reached a boiling point. "If you two don't stop talking, you'll wish you would have both been born as clams. I might be short, but I have a raging underbite that can tear into a hide quicker than you can say 'clam yourself' again. So please, shut your respective traps and stop the pacing. And Rat Dog, if you discharge another string of fire and brimstone dog farts, I'll disgorge you forever from this place."

Rat Dog was unmoved by the threat, but with the simmering heat of the early afternoon, he was in no mood to retch a retort. Daisy, on the other hand, decided to take her nervous energy outside and wait in the shade of the hedge for Dingo to return from arguing Rat Dog's case with Nemesys and the local Feeder Bowl Mangi.

A butterfly lit on her nose. This was a first for her. She'd noticed them flitting around before, but never did one land on her snout. Daisy's first thought was to snap at it, snap and crunch it just like she loved to do with cicadas. 'Ah,' she considered, 'those things make a lovely sound between my teeth, though they are a bit squishy and sour. The sound, however, is all worth it.'

On the one hand, cicadas deserved to be crunched. Their buzzing noise was utterly annoying to her, especially for a canine with such giftedly generous and sensitive ears. Butterflies, though, were of a different manufacture. Light and airy. Soundless. Graceful. Much like she was while chasing rabbits and squirrels.

After admiring it for a moment, the butterfly lifted off and flew high over the hedge. The entire experience of this event taxed her diminutive mind, and she decided it would be best to rest with ears standing erect and twitching at the slightest sound.

DAISY THE DUMPSTER DOG - A SORDID TALE OF DYSTOPIAN HUBRIS AND CONVENIENT CANINE RATIONALIZATIONS

Soon she got bored and considered heading back into the stinky lair. Then, a voice shouted out from behind her.

"Daisy?"

Being an easily spooked and timid dog, one that was accustomed to having things thrown at her by the mean standies before she found her best standies, Daisy instinctively jumped far away from the sound. Startled that anyone or anything could sneak up on her, she froze solid and rolled clumsily and stiff-legged down the incline of the hedge.

"Dingo?" she coughed, choking on the dust she'd kicked up in the commotion. "Dingo?"

"Sorry, girl," he offered. "Thought I'd sneak up on you with the good news!"

After finally gaining her bearings, she spontaneously began pogoing at his sight.

"Settle down, girl!" he urged. "Hard to tell you anything when you're leaping in the air like that." He waited for her to stop, then continued. "As I said, good news from the Feeder Bowl Mangi."

"What happened? Please, please tell me now. But wait, let's get the rest." She pranced into the lair and yelped at the top of her lungs, "Team! Dingo's back!"

BadBoy didn't stir. Nor did Dug. Nor did Rat Dog.

"He's outside?" she asked, as if it was a question and not a statement.

"Who cares?" Rat Dog mumbled. "I was in the middle of a good dream, one where the girls were admiring all that's admirable about me. Then you wrecked it."

"Tell him to come in here, as I'm not going out in the heat," Dug advised.

"Me neither," BadBoy seconded before going right back into a snore.

Although the lair would be crowded with five inside, she poked her head out through the door. "Dingo, they're napping."

"So, what's new about that?" he observed.

"Nothing," she admitted. "Come in anyway. Maybe someone besides you and me might actually care about this."

Dingo walked in and sat in front of the doorway, facing inward.

"Hey, Basenji boy!" Rat Dog complained. "You're blocking the breeze. Either get in or get out, but don't just sit there like a hound on a duck."

"What does that mean?" Daisy wondered, not understanding the reference. Not that anyone else did.

"Well," Dingo started, "I can see you're thankful that I spent the better part of my morning and afternoon arguing your case with the local Mangi and Nemesys."

Rat Dog frowned angrily and was mad enough at this interruption to raise his head off the ground. "Why should I be? I didn't ask you to do it. You concocted that entire dumpster event for your own amusement while I valiantly put my life at risk. As a positive, I got my one shot at first dib Delights, and that was my role. I could care less about your unimportant canine social morays and eels, if you get my drift. So please, removeth your butteth away from the door, or you'll discover the delicious pangs of my vicious fangs embedded in your fanny."

Daisy was growing angry. "Shut up, Rat Dog," she commanded. "Maybe you don't care. Maybe you don't participate in dogdom goings on, but I do." Then she turned to Dingo. "Please, dear friend, tell us what happened. Perhaps one of these lazy snouts will perk up an ear and listen as well."

"Your excessive, elephant-sized ears are already perked up enough for all of us," Rat Dog joked as he rested his head back onto the soft ground, ready to return to sleep in peace.

Dingo surveyed the lair. "Four pups, and only one who listens or cares," he said. "That's par for the course. When it comes to making changes for the good of society, everyone yelps loudly, but few make any effort to do anything about it. Lazy dogs. Lazy dolts. Listless dogdom."

"Indeed," Daisy seconded.

"It was a slog, admittedly," he groaned. "It wasn't as if the local Mangi had innate biases or relationships to compromise her credibility. She was a long-timer at the Feeder Bowl and gave the situation a fair evaluation. She's at least one good reason why I'm fine with local Mangi lifetime appointments. It's not like their decisions are final, by the way, and can't be appealed. Nemesys was there, of course, with a pack of special helpers to assist with his arguments. They must have been appointed by snippetty-snip higher ups in The Caste or maybe GogMad-Dog himself or themselves. But the bunch was comprised of a haughty string of purebreds and exalted ones such as you've never seen before and probably don't ever care to."

"So, were any Swatter Bowl Mangi present?" she wondered.

"I don't know. Never really seen one up close. But these dapperly decked-out doggies advising Nemesys were whispering and baying and ululating and arguing during the proceeding, much to the chagrin of the local Mangi."

Daisy wondered, "And what finally happened?"

"Well, she spit many of the weak arguments back at their wet noses. She referred to the Canistution and indicated that nothing was explicitly defined as to why The Caste needs to hold such a vaulted status over the rest of us. That was followed by more haranguing and hounding from the Nemesys pack about why its members should get first dibs at Delights and everything else in dogdom. They referred to the 'will of the Demidogs' and their old life histories, as if how those holy four-leggers lived and thought back in those days was the only thing that mattered."

"I don't get that. Why would their beloved but ancient life stories hold such importance to our lives today?" she asked innocently with a glazed look in her eyes.

He was surprised that she was still listening and comprehending a bit of it. "Okay. You asked, so here we go. Apparently, certain Mangi are bred to pretend that they can interpret the Canistution as if they were magically transported back to those days and therefore understand the original minds of the most reverend Demidogs. However, this Mangi said the plain truth is that every dog naturally comes to decisions based on their own life experiences. In other words, no Mangi can possibly possess a magical, mystical, or mysterious ability to lick the Bowl clean of their inherent biases and belief systems."

"I loved my bowl and always licked it clean," she interjected.

"Yeah," he stated, "that was a figure of speech. Despite it being impossible to come into any decision free of biases, there are some Mangi who claim to do so by regularly communing with the dead Demidogs. It's as if they're specially entitled with the bizarre and wondrous capacity to transport through time and space, reversing their canine minds backward in time. After having infused, inculcated, and impregnated themselves with those most mystical lives and thoughts; after participating in this metaphysical metamorphosis with hearts of purity and innocence; they can then claim that they alone possess and inhabit the minds of the beloved Demidogs. This therefore grants them the rightfully righteous right to apply their effulgent, unquestionable, and timeless wisdom into today's most pressing quandaries of dogdom."

"I get it," she exclaimed. "I do that with my old best standies. I think or pretend that they still miss me, and I supremely miss them. We have fun together in my mind – even though we're not actually."

He nodded. "Sure. Kind of the same. Some local Mangi have concluded that those who claim to commune with the Demidogs will very often use that as an excuse to pull the wool over our eyes. That such feigned communing gives them a convenient rationalization and veil to push forth their biases, yet yelp aloud that their own paws are clean and pure of personal prejudices. They can say they're acting as mystical channelers of the Demidogs' will. 'Heck,' she said, 'if it was that easy,

DAISY THE DUMPSTER DOG - A SORDID TALE OF DYSTOPIAN HUBRIS AND CONVENIENT CANINE RATIONALIZATIONS

such interpretation would require no prior wisdom, no life experience, and therefore no Mangi at all.' Then she concluded by saying 'it's a complete dereliction of their Mangi responsibility to bear the burden of their decisions,' though I'm not totally sure what she meant there."

Daisy, being her effervescent self, was still acting interested. "Then what happened?" she wondered.

He continued. "As relates to our situation, she explained that the Delights line-up process was never specifically, clearly, resolutely, absolutely, decisively, or doggedly defined in the Canistution. That is, it was simply a custom that expanded over multiple recent seasons, and that we should take into account the realities of today's world, a world that is far different from the ancient dog days of the venerable Demi-dogs."

Dingo's explanation had soared far over Daisy's head by now, even over her ears. In fact, this occurred when he first mentioned 'Canistution.' Regardless, she played along with keen interest, which was what she was inclined to do in almost every conversation. "So, what does that mean for us?"

"In summary," he concluded, "it means that each dog must be given equal access to Delights and equal voice in what happens around here. She said The Caste and special breeds who enjoy considerable favoritism today should not be so utterly favored. That the process of packs queuing up for Delights in a preconceived and preferential status order will need to be discontinued."

"Say what?" she queried. "If nobody lines up for Delights, if Nemesys and cronies no longer control the process, then who does?"

Dingo nodded his head. "We all do. If you go back in history a bit, you'll find that the reason a process existed in the first place was because no dog wanted a feeding frenzy anarchy to occur when the daily Delights arrived. Jumping at the opportunity to disingenuously advantage themselves, certain purebreds took control of the process in the early days. Eventually, they argued that they should stay in control simply because they were already in control. One thing led to another, and pretty soon The Caste gained more power and defined that only purebreds could hold exalted positions in the doggie dominance hierarchy and enjoy first dibs at society's treats, such as Delights. This led to them getting advantaged everywhere else. Best dibs. Best resting places. Best water access. Best bones and delicious bags of goodies."

"But we're only canines who happen to look different, right?" Daisy wondered. "Status shouldn't matter in our world."

"Of course not. But they used breeding, bloodlines, tails, musculature, fang size, and innate intelligence arguments in their narratives to separate, vegetate, and predominate us. I suppose it's natural to favor your kith and kin to a small degree, but now it's gotten way, way out of hand."

Daisy's head began to bow. "But small degree turns into large degree. I bet standies would've treated me better if my ears weren't so oversized, or if I had a fulsome tail, or if I was purebred, or if I was cuter."

"You're mega cute, Daisy," he assured her. "Look, we'll always have selfish and prejudiced thinkers and can't get away from that. But what's fair and unfair needs to be balanced out in society. That's supposed to be the job of the Mangi, especially the Swatter Bowl Mangi, to ensure dogdom is operating fairly for all, including cats. Often, however, they bark out edicts that continue to advantage the already advantaged, many who are their friends, using their Demidog mind-meld arguments as a convenient and guiltless rationale."

His stomach growling, Rat Dog finally stirred from his quasi-slumber. "Hey, limp lips. I could care less about your social yah-yah talk and more about meaningful actions and actionable meanings. Give my ears a break and net-net your travesty of blathering for us, okay? What does this imply regarding today's Delights?"

DAISY THE DUMPSTER DOG - A SORDID TALE OF DYSTOPIAN HUBRIS AND CONVENIENT CANINE RATIONALIZATIONS

Dingo smiled. "According to the local Mangi, it means everyone gets equal access to Delights from this point onward. We should be happy about that."

And happy they were, for a time.

EPISODE 327 – GUPPIES

MULTIPLE MOONS PASSED AND on this certain late afternoon, Daisy and friends had taken their new positions close to the dumpster. They were sitting patiently, waiting for Daisy to signal that she was hearing the usual activity behind the dorco door, the sounds that always resulted in Delights.

After the Feeder Bowl Mangi's edict, the local packs had been taking turns at doling out the Delights. Every dog got their fair share of first, second, and third dibs, and no canines or cats complained about the new process. Because it was fair.

Except for this day. As they waited for the dorco door to swing open, all present noticed Nemesys prancing forward with his usual gang in tow. He'd been absent around the dumpsters since the edict, and many assumed that he and his pack had simply given up, convinced to find another place where they could dominate over more docile dogs.

Not needing to partake in Delights, Dingo was absent this day. Nemesys had caught onto this fact and bullied his way to the front of the crowd, assuming his previously dominant position closest to the dorco door.

"Excuse me," Daisy politely barked. "Excuse me, Nemesys. We've established a process for equitably distributing Delights among the local packs. I don't completely understand it, but perhaps Dug can explain so that you and your friends can participate with us."

Nemesys growled angrily, "You and your pathetic four-legged freaks better back off."

DAISY THE DUMPSTER DOG - A SORDID TALE OF DYSTOPIAN HUBRIS AND CONVENIENT CANINE RATIONALIZATIONS

"Maybe you didn't hear me," she countered innocently. "We have a better, more impartial process than before. It's based on the local Mangi and Feeder Bowl edict and all that stuff. You were there when it was decided, weren't you?"

"I don't need to explain myself to you, dimwit," Nemesys spat, "but I will say this for all to hear: the most reverend Swatter Bowl Mangi have decided to make a decision to decide, for once and for all and till the end of time, to hear my case and rule in my favor. Until that event, I'm reverting back to the process that was before and what it ever should have been and will be in the future."

The crowd of canines gasped in horror. They had been told snout-to-mouth that the new process was the lay of the land. That the local Mangi decided in their favor, and that fairness and justness would rule the day. But this was a new bone thrown into the works, and Rat Dog was the first to catch on to its implications.

"Hey, you. Hey, German Shepherd-ish," he sniveled. "What is it about you that is so unlikable from a normal dog's perspective? Is it your insistence on adhering to this malicious Malinois narrative? Are you still riding that old hag? About time to give it up, little guy. Give it up, suck it up, choke it up. You're assuming that, due to your presumably reinstated status, you can boss us around? That you can recapture your unequal share? Do you believe you're the only dog in town? That your Shepherd blood is so dominant and your position so exalted, you can poop on the rest of us?"

Nemesys was surprisingly taken aback by this unexpected volley from the tiny creature, but he knew that an altercation could cost him points at the Swatter Bowl, the place where the most high Mangi made their final determinations. Rat Dog sensed this too, and he continued.

"I'm no dog psychologist, but I'd say you've got heady issues to contend with, mein Freudian Freund. Was it something dark in your past that damaged your sense of self? Did a few standies once dress you down? Did one of them place a humiliating hat on your head or make you wear a checkered vest as if you were a Scottish terrier? That would be embarrassing, no? A Scottie vest on a German Shepherd!"

A few in the crowd chuckled at his comment, further angering Nemesys and encouraging Rat Dog.

"You've been gone a bit, buddy. Did you finally locate that macho mojo you'd lost after receiving your thrashing and trashing at the Feeder Bowl? I believe I saw it lingering listlessly there by the creek, praying to find a new, more talented master who could take the reins. Wait a minute! I'm now having second thoughts. Indeed, you might look good wearing that tartan vest."

Rat Dog had fulfilled his immediate urge to disgorge and denigrate the intruder, and in the momentary silence after his last outburst, he was once again grasping for additional epithets to vomit forth. Too long a silence might lose him positioning, as he knew at this point there was no backing off, no slinking away, and no Dingo present to save his very exposed bacon.

Blister was having none of it. "Boss," he urged, "let me put him in his place and do the job I couldn't finish before. Dingo isn't here and I can make quick mincemeat of squirtville. One crunch. That's all it'll take. Fast, easy, and satisfying for both of us."

But Nemesys was considering his upcoming performance at the Swatter Bowl. He knew that it was called that for a reason: those who lacked status or import or value in society typically lost there. They were swatted ungraciously out of the Bowl, as every mangy mutt deserved to be. After his prospective win at the Bowl, he'd then have the wherewithal and high-level approval to exact his revenge on the tick, and sweet that would be.

"Back off, Blister!" he commanded. "We don't always use violence to get our way. On occasion, we use our connections, our friends in high places, and the jaws who shake our paws. We're masters at furtively chasing our chicanery behind the scenes. That's the situation in this case, so no fur will fly today. We'll have payback in the future, very soon, where we can gloat at this pathetic, deflated bloat."

"But Boss!" Blister whined. "Boss!"

"Guppies," Rat Dog snickered. "You are gutless guppies, guys. Wait until Dingo gets wind of your futile scheme."

EPISODE 328 – WOOF

MORE MOONS PASSED, AND Daisy was worried about Rat Dog's increasingly sarcastic behavior, especially how he might come off at his upcoming appearance at the Swatter Bowl. She convinced Dingo to hold a woof cart trial with her buddies to ensure that, should he be forced to speak, Rat Dog would be well-scripted. Conversely, she had no worries about Dingo's role because he was one of the smartest dudes she'd ever known.

"Okay," she began, glad that BadBoy and Dug had found sufficient value in the exercise to attend, "we're about to start."

BadBoy was indifferent. The lair was steps away, and the midday heat was bearing mightily on his thick, dusty coat. "I don't get it. Why do we need to do this activity outside the lair? It gets hot out here when you have as much tangled matte as I do."

"Same with me," Dug complained, slurping the foam from her jowls and wheezing beneath her breath. "The hotter I get, the more my mouth sudses up. Until it doesn't, which is when I die. Does everyone agree that my sorrowful fate is to die out here today in the sun?"

Dingo shook his head in disgust. This was not his vision of how a good woof cart trial should proceed. "It won't take us long, friends. We're trying to educate Rat Dog on how to comport himself before the most high Swatter Bowl Mangi, since they're a heady group of caninical types. He needs to practice what to say and not to say in the unfortunate event they request him to speak on his behalf."

DAISY THE DUMPSTER DOG - A SORDID TALE OF DYSTOPIAN HUBRIS AND CONVENIENT CANINE RATIONALIZATIONS

"So happy," Daisy exhorted, expressing her emotion at having her close friends present and in relatively good moods. "Go right ahead, Dingo."

But Rat Dog started instead. "You think I don't see what's about to happen here? Put on display like a circus act for all to ogle and get their jollies? I know nothing of this Swatter Bowl. I don't appreciate the name of it nor the implication that I'm about to get swatted. Been there, done that, and not on my list of jolly good times. Hey, Dingbat dog, are we supposed to show up on empty bellies? If so, that's a bad sign. Bad sign. You can't expect me to be at my best on legs weakened by famine. You should stop here and reconsider this purposeless plan."

Dingo was sorry he let Rat Dog trail on. "Look, pipsqueak, our efforts in the Swatter Bowl are not about you, at least not directly. They're about doing what's right for all canines versus letting the few societal favorites gain more power and status, which is what they've been doing consistently for countless moons."

But he was having none of it. "You act as if I'm stopping you, Dingbat. I keep waiting for you to ask me a question and instruct me properly. Instead, you prefer to blabber up a storm. Please proceed forth, and I'll oblige this small crowd with my overwhelming wit."

"It's not wit we're after," Dingo replied. "It's fairness. Truth. Think of it this way, nimwit. You have a good case. You were new in town; you saw things that seemed unfair to you and rightfully so to others. You spoke up and had the courage to put yourself out there, albeit in the face of getting attacked by the big dogs, the statused ones. But you stood up to them; stood up for what should be seen as a basic canine right."

Rat Dog was furious at Dingo's introduction. "Are you serious? Is this your opening statement? Truth and fairness? Are you kidding me, roborot? There's no truth and fairness that I've ever experienced. It's been 'kick him there' or 'shove him out the door' or 'he's eating the young one's food and needs to go hungry for a week to learn his lesson.'

I mean, virtually every canine I've come across has slogged this same path, and you're bringing up clean water to slurp and food bowls filled with Delights? Get real, runtola. That argument doesn't go anywhere with me and will put any peeps and pups in the Swatter Bowl to sleep. To prove my point, just look at BadBoy."

Heads turned to the overgrown mutt, who was enjoying a good slumber in the sun.

"I'm hot," Dug complained. "Think my salivating and nose running is in turbo production mode, and slurping that stuff is making me sick to my stomach. I need to leave and go do my doody, maybe an extra doody, in the usual spot."

Daisy was now exhausted with the entire effort, as was Dingo. "Geez, kids. Can't we do this one thing well? I mean, Dingo's effort to succeed is on the fast path to failure because you guys, including you, little rat, are not cooperating."

"I can't help my stomach problems," Dug confessed.

"And I'm too hot," BadBoy uttered as he slowly rose to make his way into the lair.

"I'm not worried in the least," Rat Dog bragged. "These Swatter Bowl Mangi have never seen the likes of me. Even if they don't ask me to speak, even if Dingo wants to do the yapping, I'll give them a piece of my mind regardless. Besides, I'm sure I can state my case better than the dingbat, and they'll get the added advantage of experiencing the bright light that is my enduring wisdom."

Dingo shook his head. Rarely in his long life had he felt such deep vexation and hopeless anticipation. "Daisy," he grumbled as he watched Rat Dog slink back into the lair, "I'll do my best to keep his trap shut. The runt doesn't sense the importance of this event. It's not a walk in the park for us. No way. In fact, I anticipate Nemesys will have his many favored Caste buddies and cohorts in tow. It'll be me, perched on my fours, versus him and his dastardly connections. Worse yet, the majority of Swatter Bowl Mangi are apparently affirmed advocating acolytes

DAISY THE DUMPSTER DOG - A SORDID TALE OF DYSTOPIAN HUBRIS AND CONVENIENT CANINE RATIONALIZATIONS

of the Fidoish club or clique or cadre of conniving clandestine canines and Caociphus and GogMadDog, whose admitted ambition is to advantage the already advantaged."

"I'll be there to support you, buddy," Daisy assured him. "That's probably pretty helpless help, but it's something."

EPISODE 329 – AFGHAN

THE SWATTER BOWL WAS a good distance from their lair. By the time they arrived, Rat Dog was fully spent and limping achingly on his broken leg. The pain was making him angrier with every step, as was the fact that none seemed to notice. He was in the foulest of moods as he stood to pledge support to the Canistution, which he, similar to most others in the arena, did not understand at all.

Seven mostly purebred canines were hovering over them, perched on high rock pedestals. Regally decked out in their black neck cones, Rat Dog thought they were quite the spectacle.

The Afghan among them, sporting yellow curls and recently shaved, groomed, and clipped to the nines, spoke first. "Before we commence with this dignified proceeding, we must address the obvious question as to whether this lowest of lowly caste, pudgy canines is faking his apparent leg injury. As most know, I'm not one to be dogged or otherwise hounded into a pity vote. Indeed, this deceitful display of suffering is already biasing me and a few of my colleagues against him."

Completely startled by such an indifferent and abusive remark, Dingo stumbled for a defense. Then, in a classic rookie error, he gazed across the arena and noticed many eyes, hundreds of them, focused on him. This experience was quite, quite different from the Feeder Bowl where only a few strays were sniffing around the grounds.

"Speak, idiot!" Rat Dog hissed from the small corner of his tiny snout. "You're supposed to defend me and state our case, nimbot."

Not ever having been in such a situation before, Dingo didn't realize that he suffered from large crowd stage fright. In fact, the biggest

DAISY THE DUMPSTER DOG - A SORDID TALE OF DYSTOPIAN HUBRIS AND CONVENIENT CANINE RATIONALIZATIONS

crowd he'd ever spoken before was at the instigating incident, where Rat Dog feasted to his heart's delight.

"Broken," Dingo snarled in a high pitch. And that was all he could dribble forth.

At that, Rat Dog knew his moment of valor was at hand. He needed to take control and show no remorse in doing so. Everything he had initially feared about Dingo was coming true. He wasn't a real dog, couldn't handle real dog situations, and couldn't even bark loudly enough to be heard in the arena.

Daisy was sitting right behind them, and her ears were on high alert, listening to the mumblings and rumblings and grumblings in the crowd. She held her nose high in the air to smell the smells, and there were many. In fact, it was almost impossible in this situation to rely on her for help, given the amount of energy it took to both smell and hear so much at the same time.

She looked to her left at BadBoy. He shrugged his shoulders, not knowing what to do. "I don't manage well in crowds," he sputtered, "and I heard someone comment that I stink."

Then she peered to her right at Dug. The long journey to the Swatter Bowl had burdened her body entirely. In her wheezing, snotty condition, she was in no shape to assist anyone.

But Rat Dog wasn't thinking about assistance. He was pondering how ridiculous this whole Bowl visit was, and he was about to make everyone aware of that fact.

"What are you?" he asked the Afghan, who was still waiting for the other Mangi to respond to his commentary about Rat Dog's gimp leg.

"What do you mean 'what am I?'" the Afghan rebuffed, extremely annoyed. "I'm an exalted Swatter Bowl Mangi. Perhaps you lack the mental capacity to understand your situation, and clearly this robot dog is utterly incompetent and unable to assist you. We are collectively here to assess your fragile, feeble argument to determine if it should affect anything anywhere. Probably more accurately, if it should be indelicately tossed over the fence like a steaming doggie scoop of you know what."

Rat Dog limped toward the high rocks, howling the most painful yelps he could muster as he ambled the few steps forward. "Excuse me, but did you inquire about my broken leg and whether the injury is real or not? Since you asked, I'll gladly inform this most august body. You see, I was in a big box, twelve stacks up. It was aflame and my standies left me there alone to fend for myself. My behind was searing and blistering, and I was beginning to melt. A standie far below signaled to jump, so I did and was airborne for a longer period than any canine ever. That's how I shattered my leg, in that infamous leap. Surprised you hadn't heard about it, but I suppose you're terminally cloistered and therefore unaware of much outside your own den of pups and poops. And now that I've politely responded to your question, it's customary for you to respond to mine."

The Afghan was incensed and whispered to a few of his comrades in cones, and they snorted in unison as if they'd already made their decision on his fate.

Rat Dog was incensed as well, since the Afghan had not shown him the courtesy to bark back an immediate reply. "Excuse me, big fella, but did you forget my question? I asked, 'what are you' and you responded with piddle puddle about who you were, but not 'what' you were. Would you mind answering that simple question?"

The Afghan squinted angrily at him. "I'm a purebred Afghan, if you must inquire. Bred for things you don't get and could never. I've roamed in lofty places that you can't imagine, and if you know what's good for you, you'll pay me and my colleagues our due respect."

"Due respect?" Rat Dog laughed, then hacked a bit while developing his next thoughts. "Excuse me, amigo, but I do comprehend a few things. First, your purebred breeding implies onerous inbreeding and reminds us all of the debilitating and unhealthy attributes of that. Yet your keepers just keep churning and rechurning that same corrosive

DAISY THE DUMPSTER DOG - A SORDID TALE OF DYSTOPIAN HUBRIS AND CONVENIENT CANINE RATIONALIZATIONS

set of genetic repeats and narratives to create predictable oddities like you. Second, I understand you guys engage in an unusual, unproven, and undeniable form of dog ancestor worship. I get that you are studious Canistution acolytes. But it is because you appear so gloriously studious in others' eyes that you can make or unmake, fake or head fake, take or forsake any decision you want according to your whimpering whims and convenient rationalizations. Like, maybe you caught a bad case of fleas and are in no mood to rule favorably on anything today. Or perhaps you simply don't fancy the four-legger before you or what he stands for, so you go in the yard and dig up some grift and graft about how he can't play there or anywhere else. Then you excuse it by parroting an obscure, reflective directive from Demidogs who scratched and shimmied in irrelevant ages past."

"That's it. I've had about enough of you!" the Afghan cried. "How dare you question our methods and motives! We are the Mangi Most High. Untouchable. Accountable only to ourselves. We are unsniffable and bare our butts to no lesser beings, least of all any detestable, dreadful dregs of dogs like yourself."

"Then how do you explain that oddball Fidoish club or clique or cadre of conniving clandestine canines who selected you because of your breeding, but not because you were decent and caring? Top it off with this secretive levering dude who's likely prancing around in this crowd right now. Dude's name is Caociphus and has frightful connections to," Rat Dog chuckled, "GogMadDog, apparently a very baleful batch of bowsers. I mean, get real. Will you ever speak on your own behalf, or will you always follow the stinky scent to a predictable and dreary bowl of chow that someone else put out for you? If so, then roll over and be a good boy while your trainers pull at your leash and chain and bark commands at you from behind the dark doggie door."

At this juncture, the Swatter Bowl Mangi were howling loudly as if the sky was caving in. A few of them were actively arguing to let Rat Dog continue, but the majority outbarked them. The crowd in attendance was also yelping and bellowing. It was so deafening that Daisy could no longer tolerate the noise, and she left in haste.

The Afghan was now sitting up on his two back legs to make himself appear more threatening. "I've had it with you, tiny scum runt. After briefly yapping with most of my colleagues and ethereally communing with our infusive, effusive, and obtrusive Demidog forebears, we have agreed that from this day on, across all of dogdom where we reign, all chihuahuas, rat terriers, and hybrids of such are hereby banished, completely and forever. This edict is in effect until we lifetime-appointed Mangi have seen our last days at the Swatter Bowl. And there's more. In addition to those two lowly breeds, we are also banishing all dogbots, Westies, and Westie mixes, as it appears that the large-eared one who sat behind you was your accomplice."

Rat Dog was slightly put off by such a harsh decision and surprised they took so poorly to his polite self-defense. He opened his mouth to express his feelings. "What makes you uber special that you can decide a thing such as this? Are you so insecure that you can't develop your own decisions about right and wrong? Must you instead roll and thrash about in the yard in a mock trance as if you were suddenly infused with the magical wisdom of the most reverend Demidogs and their original lives and thoughts? And who were they to have been such perfect canine masters that they could have been so prescient to have accurately envisioned these quite different dog days? No dorco or dumpster even existed in their times, isn't that correct?"

"You're out of here!" the Afghan bellowed, directing two purebred bull terriers to unceremoniously escort them from the Bowl. "And be sure they're banished forever from our sight and lands. We don't want their kind piddling on our hallowed ground."

Finally, but without remorse, Rat Dog sensed he had gone too far. Maybe they really did have the power to determine his fate, and maybe

DAISY THE DUMPSTER DOG - A SORDID TALE OF DYSTOPIAN HUBRIS AND CONVENIENT CANINE RATIONALIZATIONS

he really did step in his own dog poop this time. Upon the Afghan's last command, both he and a stumbling, mumbling Dingo were summarily swatted out of the Swatter Bowl and escorted forthwith to lands barely within smelling range of their old haunts.

"I guess that didn't turn out so well," Rat Dog surmised as he scanned the barren wasteland where they were deposited. "Had you been there for me instead of stepping on your missing tongue, things might have gone better! Think of it. We might be enjoying Delights at this moment, even if they were scraps. I'd rather have scrap than crap."

Dingo still wasn't certain what happened to his programming. It might have been a continuous loop that wouldn't stop looping, or one of those unfortunate encoding dead ends. Either way, he had no excuse.

"My sincere apologies, Rat Dog. My insides were screaming out, but my mouth wasn't moving. Never had that occur before."

In an unusual moment of kindness, Rat Dog took pity on him. "Well, you seem perfectly fine right now, but you're way too late to come to my rescue. I think you should go find a standie to locate a reset button on your metal hide. I'd bet he can also program in a personality improvement or two. You do understand that I've been in this situation before, dropped off in the middle of nowhere as the standies rolled away in their box with wheels? It's not pleasant."

Dingo was dejected but knew it wasn't the occasion to wag and wail about spilt milk. He glanced around the barren land. "Lucky for us, I have an idea where we can find refuge tonight, Rat Dog. A fair place with food. But I'm worried about my Daisy and what might have happened to her after that egregious edict. She didn't bark a single word in that Swatter Bowl, yet the Afghan laid right into her breed."

Rat Dog nodded agreeably. "He was jealous. Yeah, that's it. Jealous of me and my intellect. Jealous of Daisy because of her enormous ears or Westie parentage. I'm not sure he was jealous of you, however. He was, perhaps, concerned that you and dogbots in general are diminishing the entire canine species, especially after your listless and witless performance at the Swatter Bowl."

"Yeah. True to form. 'Swatted' is what we got and possibly what we bought," Dingo observed.

EPISODE 330 – FELINUS

"WE'RE HEADED WHERE?" RAT Dog bawled. He was beyond irate after limping all the way to the Swatter Bowl, getting booted out by the most high Mangi, and currently making a long, forced trek somewhere else. On an empty stomach, no less.

"Felinus, my friend. Felinus dos Gatos. You'll love it there," Dingo chuckled.

"You think it's funny that we were banished from our comfortable lair, that we're far distant from Delights, and are forced to live with the world's worst non-canine creatures? Indeed, roborot, your mind has been infected by a thing far more insidious than you might imagine. Do me a favor and put me to forever sleep. Terminate my rotten existence right now. The thought of me living among cats is so repulsive that I'm beyond words."

"Oh, if only that was true," Dingo wished, "my mechanical ears would finally get the rest they desperately deserve."

As they headed toward Felinus, Rat Dog caught wind of a putrefying scent. "Stop in your tracks, dogbot! We're not taking a step closer. Don't you smell that malodorous stench?"

"Smell? I sense nothing. My creators didn't bless me with a plethora of scent specifics," Dingo admitted. "What's got your complaint motor engaged this time?"

"Detritus. Sewage. Weeks old, curdled and fuzzed up milk. Ammonia. Yeah, that's it. My sniffer is overdosing on reeking, rancid, noxious ammonia. On second thought, you won't have to end it for me because I think I'm gonna die right here."

Dingo kept walking happily toward their destination. The stink meant they were close. "I assume that's cat pee and poo, my boy. Perhaps I've grown used to it."

"Used to it? Used to it? You expect me, a half chihuahua, half tar terrier, to live among cats that stink as badly as this?"

"Tar terrier?" Dingo wondered. "Thought you were a rat terrier mix. Never heard of 'tar' terriers."

"See? Do you see? The smell is so rank and file and dank and vile that I can't think straight. In fact, I'm losing control entirely. The tremors are hitting me." To amplify his point, Rat Dog stopped limping forward and began shaking all over.

Dingo laughed. "Okay. Up to you if you stop here. I understand that coyotes and racnines are out here regularly in the evening, hunting for strays and other incompetent kinds of creatures. But if you hide, say in a rabbit hole, it's equal odds that you'll live through the night. Of course, that assumes no rattlesnakes are freeloading in those holes."

"Racnines?" Rat Dog asked, still feigning the shakes. "What's that?"

"Surprised you aren't aware since you're such easy fodder for their dinner table. They're creatures the standies invented who knows when. Mixture of canines and raccoons. Devious, cunning things. They run in large packs and grow as tall as that Afghan you angered. As muscular as Blister, maybe more. And their front paws have sharp claws that can split a dog's belly open before you can cry 'ouch!' So please, stop here if you want. Felinus is just around that hill, and you'd be safe there. Likewise, you'd clearly prefer to entertain the coyote or racnine types with your cutting humor, which seems to have been very successful for you thus far today."

Rat Dog stopped shaking and sighed as he slowly limped forward to catch up. "Don't expect me to overstay my welcome. They'll not have me, and I won't have them. I'll probably expire from that painful, feline stinky-poo death, which I hear is a real sickness."

DAISY THE DUMPSTER DOG - A SORDID TALE OF DYSTOPIAN HUBRIS AND CONVENIENT CANINE RATIONALIZATIONS

"Perhaps so, ratty boy," Dingo warned, "but at least I will make it through okay. Then my ears will get that much-needed rest I keep mentioning."

It was late afternoon when the two finally made it to Felinus dos Gatos.

"Crusty, my friend!" Dingo squealed as they entered the dusty patch of scrub and water-starved trees that was home to thousands of emaciated cats.

"Heard you two got into a tussle at the Swatter Bowl," she mewed, rubbing her back up against Dingo's shoulder as if he was a scratching post. "Appears this aberrant rat made it out alive as well. And where's Daisy? Guess her kind has now been gifted with the same lowly status as our kind?"

"That's about right, Crusty," he confirmed. "This rat's mouth got us banished. Would you mind if we lodged here for a bit? Not sure how long it will be. On the flip, I've concocted a plan that might get us out of this jam."

Rat Dog had been hiding behind Dingo, pretending and hoping that he wasn't actually where he was. Dingo's comment did not go unnoticed by him. "Another plan? Similar to your last plan, the one that embarrassed me in front of the known universe and got us kicked out of dogdom permanently, as in forever? An enlightened scheme that will certainly get us back within barking distance of the dumpsters? Are you serious? And now, take a gander at this shanty town you've led us to. What a hovel! I'm being forced to live among a litter of skin-infected, flea-infested, worm-ingested felines who litter their disgusting droppings all over the ground? It's not real. I'm not having this day. Not having it."

Both Crusty and Dingo frowned at his nonstop complaining.

"I assume he's always this nasty," she observed.

"Indeed, I can't shut him up."

But Rat Dog persisted. "And the smell; how do I kill the smell, stench, stink, reek, fumes, and odors? I've heard of dogatory, a place where misbehaved canines must go at the end of their wretched days, but I had no idea it would be this bad."

As he complained, they walked past hundreds of cats, dogs and other forlorn animals who were forced to make the destitute Felinus their home. After Crusty showed them a place to spend the night, beneath an aging, half-alive eucalyptus, Rat Dog finally gave up on his incessant whining and settled in to sleep. On an empty stomach.

This reprieve from verbal abuse gave Dingo time to search for the missing Daisy. He was certain if she had gone back to the lair that Bad-Boy and Dug or worse yet, Nemesys and Blister for their own revenge, would have hastened her out of town. He was quite concerned for her safety, aware of how dangerous it was to be out in the dark beyond the confines of shelter and friends. At his request, Crusty volunteered a few residents to search the surrounding area, but as the evening wore on, they returned with no good news.

Night was falling. Rat Dog was dozing loudly, snorting with each breath, and Dingo sensed he might sleep through the night. After all, the chub was fully gimped at the end of their trek and wouldn't be going anywhere. Dingo, however, had never been out in the night alone. There were numerous hungry eyes out there, and he wasn't sure he could fight them off. A few racnines or paltry pack of coyotes might be able to take him on, he thought, but he didn't want to test out that hypothesis.

Daisy was undoubtedly in a fix. On the one hand, her ears might help keep her away from troubles in the night. On the other hand, they stood extraordinarily high up and would be nearly impossible to camouflage. One the one hand, her nose might capture the scent of oncoming trouble and help her avoid it. On the other hand, she was so gregarious and effusive that she'd likely assume everything in the dark was her

DAISY THE DUMPSTER DOG - A SORDID TALE OF DYSTOPIAN HUBRIS AND CONVENIENT CANINE RATIONALIZATIONS

friend, not foe. 'A dog of little intellect but big cheeriness,' he considered, 'which could be her undoing.'

He knew that he owed both her and Rat Dog some serious recompense for his abysmal failure at the Swatter Bowl. "I'm going out there to find her," he bayed.

Crusty was lounging above on a branch of the tree, a lizard's tail twitching from her mouth. "By yourself?" she cooed.

"Yep, by myself. You know, my creators didn't build me for emotions, and I lack fear generally and buttheadedly so. Yet Daisy and I are best friends, and I've got to save her if given the chance."

Crusty had known Dingo a long time and assumed he'd probably get up the gumption to search for Daisy in the frightful night. For her own part, she had lived a good life, albeit a hard one as a stray since birth. And the situation was getting pretty wretched for everyone in Felinus since The Caste and Swatter Bowl Mangi effectively usurped control everywhere. Besides, she felt a few of her nine were still waiting in the wings, and she didn't want to leave excess ones on the shelf before her final was utilized. "Care for company?" she asked.

Dingo peered up the tree. "No, my friend. I can't let you risk your life for this. I'll be fine."

She dropped the lizard on a branch and leapt from the tree, onto Dingo's back. "Two of us will have a better chance than one."

EPISODE 331 – CICADAS

THEY SET OFF TO search in the dark, tracing a trail backward toward the general direction of the dorco. Dingo felt there was nominal chance of finding Daisy, given the fact that neither he nor Crusty possessed useful olfactories to speak of. Worse yet, their hearing was nowhere close to what Daisy's masterful antennas could muster. Their only positive attributes were two decent pairs of eyes, but that wouldn't be of much help in an area cluttered with bramble bushes, brush, and all kinds of scary shadows lurking on the windy, moonless night that it was.

If Dingo could have shaken in fear, he would have. In fact, he was surprised his rider was so calm. "Apparently, you've been in lots of dangerous places before," he whispered as they proceeded forth into the night.

"Oh, honey," Crusty replied, "we strays encounter mortal dangers around every corner. It's in our catsblood. When sleeping, we keep one eye open and the other eye closed. One paw clawed and the other retracted. I'm ready at a moment's notice in the night for something to jump at me, or for me to jump at something. I may be getting up there in age, but at least these peepers still work pretty well. In the future, I'll regale you with my exploits, near misses, and lucky breaks. Oh, and not to worry, dearest, but I'm getting a sense that we're being stalked."

Dingo immediately halted in his tracks. "Stalked? By what? How many? Can we take them if attacked? Coyotes?"

"Settle down!" she pleaded. "Best to just keep walking and see if they follow."

DAISY THE DUMPSTER DOG - A SORDID TALE OF DYSTOPIAN HUBRIS AND CONVENIENT CANINE RATIONALIZATIONS

He strode forward a little faster than before. "Been thinking about Daisy's strongest characteristics, Crusty, though she possesses relatively few beyond her mongrel cuteness. Great ears. Great nose. However, I don't give off a smell, and she probably hasn't smelled you enough to respond if she catches a minor whiff of you."

A bit miffed at the smell comment but knowing it was the truth, she asked, "What do you have in mind?"

Dingo chuckled. "You haven't heard me try to bark, have you?"

"Can't say I have," she replied.

"She knows the sound pretty well."

"Then try it!" Crusty demanded. "What are you waiting for, a golden leash?"

At that, Dingo crouched back then let go of the loudest howl he could muster. More than a squeal, but less than a loud yelp. He tried again a few times, and the two waited in silence for an indication that Daisy might have heard it.

"Perhaps that wasn't the best decision, under the circumstances," Crusty observed. "We're notifying every night hunter in the area that a sickly dog is bawling forlornly for assistance. In fact, I'm sensing more movement to our right, and it's getting closer."

At that moment she appeared from the scrub brush, decked in scruffy white fur and covered in brambles.

"Daisy!" Dingo screamed. He jolted so quickly toward her that Crusty flew off his back and into a thorn bush.

Upon seeing them, Daisy started doing what she always did when happy: pogoing.

"Settle, girl!" he begged. "You'll awaken every coyote around."

"Coyotes?" she asked, wide-eyed and enthusiastic after catching her breath. "There are real, live coyotes out here? Can I meet one? Never seen one up close."

Crusty was busy trying to extricate herself from the bushes. "No, you can't meet one because it would have you for dinner, and not in a good way. Nor do you want to confront racnines, as these parts are rife with them. What do you say we get going since this commotion won't help our tenuous situation?"

"Crusty!" Daisy barked with joy. "You came out with Dingo to rescue me?"

"Shush!" she ordered. "We're knocking at death's door out here. Your ears standing up that high don't help either, nor your white coat, nor your unbridled display of energy. Let's head back to Felinus and safety."

"Felinus?" she wondered.

"Quiet, I said!"

After clawing free of the thorn bush, Crusty jumped onto Dingo's back for the ride home, and they began to retrace their path. Halfway there, Crusty noticed that whatever had been tracking them appeared to be dogging them closer. "Uh, um, kiddos. It's a 'don't look now' situation, I'm afraid. We have visitors in the night, at least a cat's paw full."

Dingo was immediately concerned about their chances of survival. He'd been in scuffles, but none were with coyote or racnine packs, and most were close to home. "Yep," he agreed, "let's get over to that rock outcropping. We can then face outward with the rocks to our back and claws and jaws to our front. I prefer not to be surrounded, which is what these uncivilized types are inclined to do."

So run they did, very rapidly, to the rock. It was nestled by bushes with barely enough area in front for a nasty, ugly dogfight.

"Our odds of success are slim, my friends," he stated flatly. "I make out four shadows. That's four big racnines, I think, against kind of one and a half and another half."

Daisy was standing between Dingo and Crusty, ears perked high. "You shouldn't think of yourself as half a dog, Dingo, just because you're not made of flesh."

"Not what I meant," he replied.

DAISY THE DUMPSTER DOG - A SORDID TALE OF DYSTOPIAN HUBRIS AND CONVENIENT CANINE RATIONALIZATIONS

"Besides," she continued, "if I go up and talk to them first, I'm sure we have mutual friends or amicable ways to get acquainted. Leave it to me. I'm very adept at this public relations stuff."

Crusty was annoyed by Daisy's unwitting naivete but couldn't reply. She was too busy anticipating how she might attack multiple racnines. She recalled taking on a single dog when younger. But that was one, not multiples. "Dingo, you're on the right, so you take the one crouching behind the bush on your side. I'll go for the dog on my side. Daisy, that leaves two for you, though I fear you'd have trouble wrestling a small rabbit."

"Hey, what do you mean?" She was hurt by Crusty's comment, recalling that she caught a squirrel not long ago. She thought it would continue to make sounds like those squeaky toys that she and her best standies used to play with. Only it didn't after the fourth loft in the air. "I'm a veteran hunter," she added confidently. And she was. One squirrel, a small rabbit, too many tiny lizards to recall, and lots of cicadas.

"I've handled four nasty hounds of middle size, but not four mean and hungry racnines at the same time," Dingo grunted tenuously.

They emerged from the bushes, the lead dog growling fiercely and displaying its fangs and lengthy front claws.

"Claws?" Daisy questioned aloud. "How cool! Hey guys, my name's Daisy..."

At that, the dog, cat, dogbot, and racnine fight began in a rolling furball of wails and whines. In the middle of the fracas, Daisy glanced at Dingo. His left leg appeared nonfunctional, and he gave her a 'we tried' wink. Crusty, too, was looking the worse for wear. All Daisy could think of was her best standies playing with her in the yard, throwing the squeaky toy, catching it in the air, and teasing her standie to pull it from her jaws when she brought it back. 'In fact,' she considered, thinking it would be her last thought, 'I'm now positive that's how I lost those front teeth.'

Just when it appeared they'd be served as that night's meal of broken parts for hungry racnines, something unexpected happened.

Blister appeared out of nowhere. He jumped from atop the rock outcropping right onto the lead racnine's head, his mouth wide open. Having gotten ahold of its neck, he then launched the dog high over the bush. As it crashed to the ground, the other three racnines heard a sorrowful squeal. They quickly stopped fighting and scurried away.

"Guess that was his call to retreat," Blister boasted.

In normal circumstances, Daisy would have begun bounding up and down, pleased to see Blister approach. Though her heart wanted to, her left hindquarter didn't. It had a wide gash that was dripping blood. Crusty had a few scrapes as well but came out of it less damaged due to her years of experience. And Dingo, poor Dingo, sustained a damaged and nearly useless back leg.

"Blister!" Daisy yelped happily, still not aware of how painful her injury was. "So glad to see you! Where's Nemesys and your friends? I had to leave the Swatter Bowl early."

"Daisy!" Dingo interrupted. "Not the occasion for greetings and salutations. We must get back to Felinus to lick our wounds, and pronto."

"How come you showed up to save the day?" Crusty inquired as they started the journey back, very slowly.

Blister wasn't accustomed to talking with cats. He'd only ever done it a few times. In fact, he usually spoke only with Nemesys, and that conversation was always about how he should do this or that, or how he wasn't acting properly for his lower status, or how he needed to be smarter. He wasn't sure how to respond to Crusty, so he turned to Daisy.

"To be honest, I went to your lair to kick you out of town according to the edicts, rulings, wishes, and mandates of the vaulted Swatter Bowl Mangi, but you weren't there. I asked BadBoy and Dug where you wan-

DAISY THE DUMPSTER DOG - A SORDID TALE OF DYSTOPIAN HUBRIS AND CONVENIENT CANINE RATIONALIZATIONS

dered to, and they pointed in this general direction. By the way, this is about as close as I plan to get to Felinus."

"You're heading back in the dark?" Dingo questioned with eyebrows raised.

"I suppose. If I got scared easily, I wouldn't be out here. Been known to hold my own in worse situations."

"Why do you do it?" Daisy asked innocently.

Blister cocked his head to the side. "Rescue you? I'm not sure. Didn't care to see the racnines win, I guess."

"Well, that too," she said. "But why do you do it, meaning why do you act as a lap dog for Nemesys? Is it the food and toys? That stuff wouldn't be adequate for me, honestly. Of course, your reputation isn't the greatest among the lowly four-leggers, which includes most dogs everywhere. Perhaps self-respect doesn't mean anything to you?"

This got Blister going. "Look, Daisy, you're lucky I was in such a good mood. I'm telling you, it's not easy doing what I do, fighting someone else's fight. I haven't really thought of what it means for me. I get what I get from it. Decent food, shelter, and status. If certain whelps don't take to me, then they're jealous. Maybe."

"Or maybe not," Crusty added, as they continued walking. "Maybe you don't actually like what you do, and you can't face your reflection in a pond and feel good about who you are. You're part of a scheme that perpetuates the fortunes of the fortunate few at the expense of the multiple downtrodden."

"Well," he observed, "I don't care much for cats, but then I haven't known any up close. I suggest that you must stay away from places where The Caste is in control or the Swatter Bowl Mangi hold sovereign authority."

"And why is that?" she purred.

"Because The Caste avails and advantages its own, as you just indicated. You guys are presently lower than bat guano in their eyes. Possibly for good reasons, but probably not. And if not, I have no clue how to stop their madness. It's too embedded in them, as if it's their dog-given, dog-granted, dog-endorsed birthright. Then their self-told narratives are reinforced by their murky, dirty handlers who pretend they have complete control of their choke collars. I can't say that I'm pleased with what's happened lately. In fact, I've heard talk that there could be further restrictions on canine freedoms around the bend."

"What does that mean?" Dingo wondered. "More restricted breeds?"

Blister nodded. "Better said as 'more breed restrictions.' Many of us will worry that this last insufferable set of edicts against Westie and Westie mixes, for example, could spill over to any breeds that dare bark against them. Geez, they might even ban Boxers next. There are quiet rumblings about the Swatter Bowl Mangi and The Caste and the pukey bile that's regurgitated in dark places to elevate them into their lofty positions. These bile types are not concerned about doing the right things for us or any animals, for that matter. It's far more about advantaging themselves and their butt-sniffing buddies, then finding ways to further dominate and profit from the less fortunate."

Dingo smirked, then stopped limping for a second and turned to him. "Interesting to hear you admit to this, Blister. I always assumed you were part of the cultish lot that these packs run with, and that you enjoyed the perks the sordid game offered you."

He shook his head in disgust. "No. As one of the lowest in this menagerie of highbrow sniffers and performing the muscle role, it's not a great place to hang your collar. Hierarchical. Domineering. Condescending. Unjust. Authoritarian, even. I don't condone the worship of certain canines solely because others worship them. In reality, we're all simply dogs trying to make our way."

"And cats," Crusty added.

"I suppose cats should get an equal vote," he admitted, "but everything is disequal now and growing more so."

"Unequal, you mean," Dingo corrected him.

DAISY THE DUMPSTER DOG - A SORDID TALE OF DYSTOPIAN HUBRIS AND CONVENIENT CANINE RATIONALIZATIONS

"No. I said what I meant. 'Disequal.' It's a portmanteau, a merging of two words or concepts."

"Of course!" Daisy whooped. She was elated to hear the word again and couldn't stop wagging her stub.

He continued. "It's a combination of 'diseased' and 'unequal.' Disequal. For example, here's what I've been hearing around dogdom: 'If the Swatter Bowl Mangi can so utterly disregard rules that have been in place for so long, rules about how canines and even cats should be treated fairly, then the majority of them must have gone rabid.'"

"Rabid?" Daisy knew this was a bad word.

"Yes. Not rabid physically. Rabid in their minds. That's a worse ailment because they're not obviously frothing at the mouth. The froth is in their heads, and we four-legged types are rarely adept at catching such subtle inferences. It doesn't bode well for canines since the Swatter Bowl Mangi are the sole, lone, and singular power structure remaining to prevent us from devolving into dogarchy where the unlucky few survive."

"Geez," Daisy observed, "the poor canines. Such weighty harnesses on their shoulders!"

Blister chuckled sadly. "Nothing poor about them or how many of these doggedly disqualified and unqualified Mangi got hastened, shoved, booted, boosted, and launched into those vaulted and exalted positions. Most have it good; very good. They prefer to ignore the shantytowns of strays and misfits. Instead, they commune only with Caste friends in the safety of their guarded doghouses and play yards. 'Insular' is the relevant word, I believe. They're out of touch. Topping it off, they're given lifetime appointments. Imagine enjoying always filled bowls and constant, stroking attention by both their handlers and disciples. Oh, and that reminds me."

"Of what?" Dingo asked.

"An unsettling rumor," Blister confided. "Apparently, some of the Swatter Bowl Mangi are taking advantage of these lifetime job appointments, especially considering how short our poor canine lives are."

Crusty was tiring of the snout chat and wanted to get back to the comfort of her tree. "Please, cut to the chase. We're nearly home."

"Well," he whispered, "rumor is that they're pouring more than just kibble in their bowls. Insiders say that certain of them are ingesting Ponce pills and powders to make them live longer. Maybe a lot, and perhaps forever. Imagine that: overflowing bowls of fresh water and wonderful food; warm beds; canines drooling and prostrating themselves at your mere presence. And all you have to do is wolf down these Ponce pills and powders to get that goodness for dogternity? Like having your cake and eating it, too. Again, forever."

Daisy was otherwise absorbed at licking her wound, but her attention picked up at the mention. "Cake's my favorite."

Dingo pondered for a moment, then spoke. "I've heard that rumor before. If it's true, such a thing could disrupt the entire hierarchy, Caste, and lifetime appointments. Imagine, a small cult of canines with exalted status, forever able to reign over dogdom and its inhabitants?"

"It's bad enough living the humiliating way we do, below the lowest rungs on the dominance pole," Crusty moaned. "But for this to go on forever and ever because a few majestic ones were granted high status along the way? Just not right."

Dingo nodded. "That's the dogtopian pyramid of pyramids. Where they never die, never tumble from the apex, and retain hot dog, top dog, big dog status forever? It's disgusting that it could come to this, but we'll have to ponder the implications later. For now, we're getting close to Felinus. Blister, I suggest you don't return until daylight."

"What's that horrible smell?" he gagged. "Ammonia? Even with my smashed nose, I can still whiff that stink. I'm not going in there; no way. This is too close. I'll find a place to park out here tonight, then head on back when it's light again."

DAISY THE DUMPSTER DOG - A SORDID TALE OF DYSTOPIAN HUBRIS AND CONVENIENT CANINE RATIONALIZATIONS

The four of them stopped for a moment, and Daisy walked up to nudge his shoulder. "Thanks, Blister. We owe you a treat or two."

"Don't mention it," he replied. "And I mean exactly that. Tell no dogs that I intervened or relayed this stuff. Nemesys would squat on my hide before blistering poor Blister with a blister pack. And I don't know who I'd be if I lost my status."

"A nice dog with a calm sense of dignity and pride, perhaps?" Dingo remarked.

EPISODE 332 – BITER

EVEN MORE MOONS HAD passed since their appearance at the Swatter Bowl, too many for Rat Dog to recall. He remained in a very bad mood with visions of his one big moment, his only chance at first dibs, replaying in a continuous loop in his tiny mind.

Missing their lair mates, Dug and BadBoy decided to visit their old friends in their new home in Felinus. The six of them, including Crusty up in the tree, were evaluating the status of things.

"We've heard increased bellowing lately among our fellow riffraff," Dug observed. "The Swatter Bowl Mangi are issuing a host of new edicts on canine freedoms and restrictions thereon. We think it's because they were brutally embarrassed by the entire Rat Dog episode. Since then, they've become more aggressive and hard-lined. Thanks personally to you, Rat Dog." She glowered intently at his beady eyes.

Rat Dog was accepting none of the blame. "Me at fault? I asked a few questions. A few, simple, straightforward questions about how and why they're so inflexible and dogmatic in their beliefs. I mean, the whole audacious act of communing with Demidog ghosts and getting inside their minds? Really? Shows how most are entirely out of step with life today. It wasn't my fault. I'm the innocent messenger dog who's gotten shot here."

"No," Dug countered. "You're guilty on all counts, and the permanent ban on chihuahuas and rat terriers is indicative of their anger. Geez, they even expelled purebred Westies, Westie mixes, and dogbots. Worse yet, they and The Caste are sniffing the ground and sending out

DAISY THE DUMPSTER DOG - A SORDID TALE OF DYSTOPIAN HUBRIS AND CONVENIENT CANINE RATIONALIZATIONS

their dog catchers to collar any poor whelp who dares to speak against them."

"My point exactly," Rat Dog spat back. "I'm fine with prohibiting certain breeds, but they picked the wrong ones! For instance, they should have banned dog types where you can't tell if they're coming or going. You obviously understand, Dug. Flat-nosed and fail-tail breeds like yourself."

BadBoy growled angrily. "Enough, tick, or I'll launch your portly pudge right over this tree."

He didn't flinch. "Might as well. My life has effectively ended, thanks to each of you. It reached a very short-lived zenith when I got first dibs, and now I'm in the lowest possible place and having to tolerate this constant burning sensation in my olfactories. How the mighty have fallen! To top it off, I'm allergic to cats." He then feigned a sneeze.

"Nobody cares for your complaints," Crusty commented from the tree above. "You always have the option to bug out on your own and join a pack of coyotes or racnines. They'd love to have you for a meal."

"Ha ha ha," he laughed in jest. "Do you know how often you've repeated that joke since I arrived?"

"We're not getting anywhere, kids," Dingo observed.

Daisy was concerned with none of this and was so excited that her friends were all in one place. "As long as we have each other, that's what I care about. Smell or no smell, and I have a great nose, both Crusty and Felinus have been wonderful hosts to us."

"Thanks, Daisy," she replied.

Rat Dog's head shook in disgust. "We're getting nowhere because everyone prefers to sit around like docile dogs and instinctively bark their heads off, as if that's going to change our sorry situation. Did you see me doing that when I heroically jumped from the flaming box and splintered my leg? Did you see me wilt like a fragile flower before the Swatter Bowl Mangi, as another canine here in our midst did? No. Not me. I was the selfless one who valiantly stood up for us poor pooches while enduring endless pain in my leg. Bearing my butt publicly for the benefit of all others. I was the one who put the Swatter Bowl blue bloods in their place and forced them to reconsider their doggone purposes in life."

"Which again leads to how depraved and disgusting our situations have become since Rat Dog spouted off at the Swatter Bowl," Dug interjected. "Not saying it was his fault entirely, as The Caste and their ilk are primarily to blame. But we've had so many edicts issued so quickly across so many areas for the benefit of so few. It's a 'dogs running wild' situation now. We're tired of nodding our heads about how bad things are. There's increasing scuttlebutt that we downtrodden mutts should actively parade and protest in the streets to restore our rights and repair the system."

BadBoy finally added one key observation of the whole mess. "Can't hope to repair the system, though, when the supposed, prophetical visions of the original Demidogs are regurgitated in every decision where it's convenient for the Swatter Bowl Mangi to do so, while these same visions are not disgorged when it's not convenient."

As he completed his comment, Daisy's elephant ears perked straight up, and everyone couldn't help but notice. "I hear new pawprints at the edge of town," she observed.

The new pawprints were from a visitor who was escorted by one of Crusty's furtive friends to the spot where the crew was conversing at the tree. Daisy started springing high in the air at first sight.

"Greetings!" she howled, finally calming herself sufficiently to give others a chance to meet the visitor without risking an unfortunate body slam as she descended. "Who are you?"

Crusty's friend announced her. "Mystery guest. Appears she's looking for Dingo the dogbot. Since this is the only metallic dog in Felinus, I figured it would have to be him."

DAISY THE DUMPSTER DOG - A SORDID TALE OF DYSTOPIAN HUBRIS AND CONVENIENT CANINE RATIONALIZATIONS

Crusty considered the occasion momentous enough to leap from her tree to the ground. "Sorry about the mixed-up Westie mix, my friend. I'm Crusty, one of the cool cats in charge of this place. We tend to be pretty territorial, so this is my ground. However, strangers are always welcome."

The others, except for Rat Dog, introduced themselves accordingly. The visitor still hadn't barked a word, but the crew was busy admiring the sheer beauty of her gray-brown coat and friendly face.

"What are you?" Rat Dog insisted, voicing his typical greeting to gain the smallest advantage.

She stared firmly at him, as if she'd encountered his scrawny face before. "A dog. And you?" she replied.

He wasn't accustomed to immediate retorts like this. "Ah, I can see you're a bit slow. That's okay. I'm not asking if you're a dog. We have eyes. We get that. I'm asking a question that any sane canine would ask when inquiring about the obvious. Again, what are you?"

Then she realized what he meant. "Oh! You must mean what my breed is. I'll tell you. I am half Australian shepherd and half Australian stumpy tail cattle dog."

At the mention, Daisy began pogoing again. Yes, this dog's tail was half-formed, which made her conclude they had both suffered the same fate when young. She began babbling and yipping with such exuberance that they could hardly understand her.

"Did the standies cut your tail off for the same reason that mine did? From what I recall, they clipped my tail when I was just a pup. Long ago. Despite the pain, I saw them put it in one of those very frigid boxes, the kind that pours cold air on you when they open it. I'm sure they're using my tail for secret breeding purposes. You'll notice right off that something is totally different, scientifically advanced, about me. Look at my ears, for example. Have you ever seen ears as useful as these? I believe the standies created me like they did with Dingo, but I was flesh and he was metal. They were probably experimenting with deer or rabbit ear features and put them into me, and I occurred as a result. I assume they wanted to create a Westie with superior hearing. My sense of smell is also outstanding, and your scent seems familiar to me. Either way, to conclude on this interesting story about myself, it's clear the standies have been using my tail for important things such as experiments or to create more versions of me for others to enjoy. I'll confirm that when I find another canine lookalike, or maybe a rabbit or deer with Westie features. Given that this exhilarating story explains the mystery of my bobbed tail, what's your story?"

All were completely stunned for a moment. Rat Dog was speechless at Daisy's extended, loony rant. Dingo felt the need to insert a break into such an embarrassing pause. "Thank you, Daisy. As I indicated, my name is Dingo. We didn't get your name."

"Wait a minute! Wait a darn minute!" Rat Dog insisted. "I don't care about her name. She didn't properly respond to my first inquiry. Then Daisy went hog wild to our great misfortune, speaking in unintelligible dog tongues, and all present conveniently forgot that I politely asked this newcomer a question and expect an answer." He then peered at her menacingly with his steely bug eyes. "Do you even know what you are?"

She was nonplussed by Rat Dog's continued rudeness but seemed pleasantly annoyed, as if she'd encountered deviant pups similar to him in her past. "I'm Australian...," she began again.

Only, Rat Dog didn't let her. "Hold it right there!" he interrupted. "Can't be. Hey, I've come across more than a few Australians in my day, and you look nothing like them. They were meaty and tough, at least when I sank these large fangs into their whiny behinds. I'd say you're about as Australian as Dingo. And where's the accent, if so? I mean, who'd want to claim they're Australian in these parts? We understand that a paw full of awful Aussies are responsible for the sad state of the canine world today and for the world in general. I've heard tell that they screwed the pooch for everyone. Life was apparently much better many moons ago and still would be, but for them."

"Quiet!" Dug demanded. "Speaking of rants, you're the most ranty, shanty dog that's ever walked this ground. Give the poor girl a little breathing room and shut that snapper before I lunge at your hide."

"Please, no violence!" the visitor insisted. "I'm afraid canines, cats, and all forms of sentient creatures are scurrying around a bit too hot these days. Cooler heads must prevail, or pooches and every cat or mouse or grouse or louse will suffer. Please, call me Biter, as my closest friends do."

Rat Dog was incensed that any self-respecting dog would take that name. He was the biter and a renowned master at that art. "Biter? Seriously? You're so insecure about your ability to defend yourself that you named yourself 'Biter' to warn others, despite your obviously weak and flaccid jawline? I'm looking up there, and the fangs appear rounded off and harmless. In contrast, take a gander at these sharp babies!"

As Rat Dog bared his tiny fangs, the others burst out in laughter.

"Thanks," BadBoy mumbled, still chuckling. "I hadn't had a good laugh since the Swatter Bowl Mangi edict that drove my friends away. Really needed a moment of humor to kick me out of this funk."

Biter was not letting this go, either, adding, "Living proof that the size of one's mouth is often inversely proportional to the fetid sludge that issues from it."

That got a greater response from the crew, excepting Rat Dog, of course, who was busily trying to understand what she meant.

"Why have you come to visit, my friend? Did someone refer you to me?" Dingo inquired.

She hesitated momentarily, then let it slip. "First, I confess to not having visited Felinus in moons. It's easy to forget where you came from and conveniently pretend that all animals have access to treats, toys, and great shelter like I do. To pretend is to ignore and to assuage one's guilt by brushing away the thoughts. But to answer your question, I noticed you at the Swatter Bowl, Dingo. I was among the canines in attendance, and perhaps that is why Daisy recalls my scent."

The mention of the Bowl got Rat Dog more agitated just as he was settling down. "You saw Dingo there? You observed his miserable carcass in inane and indiscreet inaction? Well, I guess that's all you could have done, considering that he didn't do a positive thing beyond consume space!" he groaned. "This uber-talented robotic fiend caught a bad case of heartwormed stage fright and failed to whimper a word of defense on my behalf. Lucky for me, though, I'm a veteran at strutting my stuff. I marched right out before the Mangi and the ravenous crowd that were wailing and gnashing teeth to advance my demise. There, I stated my position more effectively than any dog might have dreamed."

"And dream it remains," Dug added. "A dream that you actually won your case and spoke eloquently for the downtrodden. Instead, you were so categorically rude and despicable to the Mangi that you got yourself, Dingo, and Daisy chased completely out of town on your hind legs. Most would consider that one very doomed and defeated dog day afternoon."

Her astute remark was enough to cause Rat Dog to finally back off. He lowered his ears and slinked to the rear.

Biter was chomping at the bit to speak and felt that this was finally the right moment to express herself without his painful interruptions. "I've come on behalf of myself and friends. I can't impart more about me, unfortunately, but I will say that your visit to the Bowl has amplified certain discomforts in society that have been pushed aside for too long. Perhaps you've heard of the growing disquiet among the lower classes of canines."

"Don't forget cats," Crusty interjected.

"Yes, we heard that fairly immediately after their edict that pushed us out the door," Dingo added.

"Indeed," she confirmed, "and things are growing worse. The Caste and Swatter Bowl Mangi are tightening control, issuing more edicts

DAISY THE DUMPSTER DOG - A SORDID TALE OF DYSTOPIAN HUBRIS AND CONVENIENT CANINE RATIONALIZATIONS

to favor the previously and persistently favored, like fleas on a hound's butt. I fear the situation is becoming untenable. Then we have the followers of the Fidoish club or clique or cadre of conniving clandestine canines continuing to groom, inculcate, and indoctrinate new pups to unquestioningly wolf-down their exceedingly narrow viewpoints. This creates a steady supply of trained attack dogs who are no more than zinging zealots that regularly spout their simplistic and singular perspectives. And I can't forget to mention Caociphus, their progenitor, and the shadowy and sinister GogMadDog who provides them with endless fronting and backing. A real den of antiquity and iniquity has wrested control over dogdom, I fear."

Without getting noticed, Rat Dog crawled forward and was nearly situated in the middle of the circle of discussion. He wasn't taking her commentary well. "Den? As in wolves? Do you think I care about hapless and helpless wolves and such? Didn't you hear that I recently fought off a vicious multitude of racnines because I courageously volunteered to search for Daisy in her most desperate hour?"

"Shut it!" Crusty growled. "Dingo, Daisy, and I faced them while you were sleepy dreaming under this tree."

"Whatever!" he exhorted. "I fear no wolves or racnines. Do you know your problem, lady?"

Biter remained appalled at his continuing rudeness but tried to take control of the conversation. "Yes, I'm very aware."

"I think not," he countered. "Your problem, and the problem with all lowly canines who love to prevaricate in their precious little societies and gatherings and groupings about how to fix things, is that you don't have a plan, don't have a strategy, and don't persistently execute on anything. Not me, but some would call that cowardice. You lack the gumption or energy or courage to counter this Caociphus or GogMadDog or Caste. Nonetheless, you'll whine, whimper, and cry constantly about how unfair things are, and hope your forlorn exhortations will magically resolve your predicaments."

He stopped momentarily to inhale a deep breath. Dingo let out an audible sigh, anticipating what might come next. And it did.

"Well, guess what? They don't. They exacerbate them. You assume that in barking your complaints, then barking louder, a few courageous and energetic hounds will miraculously emerge from the fog and doggedly fix the things that you're too lazy or indifferent to repair yourselves. But it ain't so. Your problem is your niceness and politeness and agreeability. When you're fighting a den of wolves or racnines or coyotes, you'd better buckle up, buddy, and prepare for battle. You'd better get smart and outsmart them. A good offense is the best defense. Think I was the first ever to say that. But you guys don't understand offensive, aggressive play. You'd rather romp and jump around and pretend as if you're top dog than actually be the top dog. Wimpy pups, the lot of you, always get wimpy results, so runts of the litter you will remain. You make believe that you live in a dog utopia, but you don't. It's a dogstyopia."

"What's that?" Daisy asked innocently.

"I told you a while back. It's a portmanteau," he replied in disgust.

"Oh, I get it!" she yelped joyously. "You mean a combination of 'dog' and 'dystopia,' right?"

"Oh boy," he grumbled, "at least you're learning, but you're not entirely right, as expected. It's a combination of three words: dog, stye, and dystopia. Have you ever suffered from a stye in your eye? Holy stick, I had one some moons back and knew I was gonna die from it. I might have, in fact, but that subtle power within managed to spark me back to life. Lucky for you all, I'm here today."

During this back and forth, Dingo was trying to assess why such a canine would have the interest to mysteriously appear, ask for him, and provide her thoughts on the status of canine society. Rat Dog's tirades gave him time to think and consider all that he'd heard, including Blister's comments.

DAISY THE DUMPSTER DOG - A SORDID TALE OF DYSTOPIAN HUBRIS AND CONVENIENT CANINE RATIONALIZATIONS

"Biter," he began, "we generally ignore this little tick's comments, but he has a good point for once in a moon. You must ask yourself how we allowed it to get to such an imbalanced state. How could these purebreds take over society and perennially lead our packs by the nose? As Rat Dog said, it must be because we let the void happen. Think of raw meat that magically appears every day in the middle of an arena and all are sitting some distance from it. Then, a few are sly enough to erect a plan to capture the meat and keep it for themselves and those they favor, while the others don't have a plan and go hungry instead. So, who should win this dogfight, and should winner take all?"

BadBoy harumphed. "Thanks for reminding us. You just described the dorco situation."

"It seems complex," she answered, "but it's not. Admittedly, The Caste and its ilk indeed have a significant head start. They began planning earlier and determined how to create a tiered society that favors themselves and disfavors all else. A true dog-eat-dog mentality where they are currently and forever will remain the top dogs. And it's not truly about being purebred, though they use that as an excuse for what they do. Purebred is not genetics; it's only a state of mind. They're experts at pressing this narrative into our infirm and hungry minds, making us believe they have a righteous and virtuous rationale for always getting the best of every meal while we should be so lucky to savor the few morsels that remain."

"Yeah. Like who gets first dibs on dumpster Delights," Rat Dog moaned.

"Yes," she said, surprised that he actually added to the conversation. "They tell you they must get first dibs because you've given them the power to tell you that. You've conceded, we've conceded, to their views of societal dominance. I can't say I admire the way Rat Dog barked it out, but he is right for once, Dingo. Most of us get too enmeshed in our everyday lives, foraging for the bits and scraps of life and considering little else beyond our next meal. We take our eye off the ball when it's thrown. We let the few devious and designing ones, the purebreds and Caste and Swatter Bowl Mangi in this case, control our lives. They push false narratives that they're graciously giving us freedoms, when they're actually taking them away. They claim that they're magically infused with the mystical minds of the Demidogs, our perfectly imperfect founders from ancient days. Then you'll find them rolling and thrashing about in a vast, archaic grassland of vague interpretations when it advantages them to do so. Their 'Demidogs interpretation narrative' also provides them with a convenient excuse to wash their claws of responsibility for their decisions. Any forthright fourlegger can readily track down the cunning cowardice and fragile funk of that thinly veiled pawsible deniability argument."

"Including the decision to ban Westies and Westie mixes and dogbots?" Daisy wondered.

"Yes indeed, antenna ears," Rat Dog confirmed, "but you forgot to mention the highest of breeds: rat terriers and chihuahuas."

Biter added, "With many more restrictions to come for additional breeds, as well as freedoms we've historically enjoyed."

Dingo was anxious to get to her purpose, which had not yet been uncovered. "Why did you risk coming all this way to Felinus to tell us what we pretty much knew, particularly after our failure at the Swatter Bowl?"

"It was your failure alone," Rat Dog argued.

"All right. My failure," Dingo confessed.

Biter began to stand, a signal that she had to leave. "Yours was a failure of sorts, but that's how we learn survival. If you don't try, you don't fail. If you don't fail, you don't learn. I came here to inform you that your 'failure' has caused quite a stir. Of course, you can't return there yet, and perhaps this concern will blow over, considering that dogdom tends to raise lazy and listless pups in general."

DAISY THE DUMPSTER DOG - A SORDID TALE OF DYSTOPIAN HUBRIS AND CONVENIENT CANINE RATIONALIZATIONS

Beyond occasionally putting Rat Dog in his place, Dug had been unusually quiet. "Cat's got your tongue?" Dingo inquired, noticing how pensive she was acting.

"Maybe so," Dug admitted. "I sense there's more you wanted to tell us, Biter. You might regret not having said it."

Lifting his head from a prone position, BadBoy wanted to make everyone aware that he'd also been actively listening. "Dug's got that right, you know."

Biter took a deep breath. "Well, I was weighing whether to mention this or not, but I'm being coaxed for the truth. There's increasing chatter in high circles that certain Swatter Bowl Mangi are ingesting Ponce powders and pills to extend their lives."

"I understand why," Crusty observed. "All canines should hope to possess nine lives like us. It seems quite unfair if they acquire them unnaturally, however."

"Very unfair," Biter agreed. "I believe you'll come to the same conclusion that I've arrived at on this topic. The Swatter Bowl Mangi, those lucky canines who've already been gifted with lifetime jobs at the loftiest level, might now live forever. Certainly far longer than they do now as unadulterated adult purebreds, which is far longer than what the ancient and long-dead Demidogs ever perceived possible."

"What's unfair about that? Kind of cool, if you ask me," Daisy remarked.

Biter thought not. "What's uncool is that the Mangi were granted lifetime jobs from the Canistution. But that was decided long ago, when canines lived brief and dangerous lives. Back then, a rational dog could rationalize that it was okay to grant them such guarantees because doggie lifetimes were extremely short. They logically assumed that Swatter Bowl Mangi would be continually cycled out, with old ones dying and new ones taking their place. Nobody foresaw that a few individuals might be able to effectively rule over dogdom forever. It's too bad that we all can't commune with the venerable but really dead

Demidogs to determine if that was their intended and intentional intent!"

Dug laughed at her levity, then asked the obvious question, "Why were they given lifetime jobs in the first place?"

"It was a hope, a lark, an incisive and now derisive decision by the Demidogs. The idea was that Swatter Bowl Mangi held such extensive power that they might use it inappropriately to favor certain of society's top dogs. They concluded that if the most high Mangi were consistently booted out after some time to fend for themselves, certain of those conniving societal top dogs might potentially ply and cajole and shower and promise them with bowls of cake and honey after their Mangi jobs were over. In other words, they assumed those incorruptible Mangi might indeed be corruptible and corrupted, given the right offer. Therefore, the well-intentioned but not necessarily faultless Demidogs concluded that the only way to prevent such undue influences was to grant every Mangi a job for life, or at least whatever they meant by the term 'lifetime' at that ancient time."

Biter paused for a moment to ensure that she was making sense. Daisy, for her part, was vigorously chewing away at her front paw, completely oblivious. But Biter continued on.

"Funny, when you think of it, that they were worried about devious top dogs having too much influence over the Swatter Bowl Mangi, so they gifted the Mangi with lifetime jobs. In a wickedly doggonic and ironic twist of fate, the polar opposite of what the Demidogs intended has actually occurred. A majority of the Swatter Bowl Mangi frequently issue edicts in favor of the same top dogs in The Caste. And why not, since most Swatter Bowl Mangi regularly chum around with them in the same purebred packs? Besides, many are either active or former sporting or working or herding members of the Fidoish club or clique or cadre of conniving clandestine canines. This has resulted in a causal cloud of ingrained graft and corruption that could never have been anticipated by the revered founders. Topping this off, these Ponce-pow-

DAISY THE DUMPSTER DOG - A SORDID TALE OF DYSTOPIAN HUBRIS AND CONVENIENT CANINE RATIONALIZATIONS

dered Mangi are now poised to roust and regale and rule and rust far into the foreseeable future, which is very long."

Crusty rubbed up against Dingo and scratched her chin on his gimp leg. "This means cats will never, ever get fully integrated into society. We'll perpetually lurk and scurry in the dark and dingy haunts of Felinus, and at best get the fishbone pickings of entitlements like dorco Delights."

"And we non-preferred, lowly, and inconsequential canines will remain on the low rungs because The Caste and their buddies will have the everlasting power to make it stay that way," Dingo squeaked.

Biter was shuffling backwards and started to turn away from the crew. "We appear to be headed on the path that social structures take before they doggedly and dastardly decline. It's these consanguineous relationships, the inbreeding of siblings and cousins, that have created vexatious weaknesses in our species. In this case, however, the irrecoverable consanguineous relationships are ones of fanatical, inflexible, and intolerant thought, all sheathed in fervent, ferocious, self-serving, and self-righteous narratives. Consider The Caste and their ilk who regularly hack up hairballs of deceitful dogma to ensure they never lose power or special entitlements. Alas, such narrow-minded societies will fail for the same reasons they always have: they keep propagating and repeating the same insular thoughts and can't adapt as a result. Insular is the easy trail and therefore the deadly dangerous one. They incessantly regurgitate their own biases and harshly held belief systems, then attempt to force every dog to slurp-up their narratives on command, right from the bowl of worm-infested gruel. Should that be a dog's life?"

As Biter backed away, she offered one last thought. "Don't get me wrong. It's easy to complain about such zealots because they seem ultra-pigheaded. However, the problem is not simply with them. It's with us. There will always be racnines and coyotes and Fidoish clubs or cliques or cadres of conniving clandestine canines and similar extremists trying to reinvent dogdom in their favor. That's reality. But if we fail to actively chase down and capture any of our own plans, any of our own dogma, or any counterattacks to their constant hounding? Then they'll control everything, including the dorco Delights of which Rat Dog speaks so fondly, and we will well-deserve the nasty bones and scraps that get tossed at us in the end."

She turned to leave, then peered back with a questioning look. "I meant to ask you, Crusty. What's that huge bird doing in your tree? I find it odd that any winged ones would find a comfortable perch in Felinus, given the not-so-amicable history of your respective species."

"Ah," Crusty replied, "you mean my eagle friend. She landed here some moons ago. Going blind, unfortunately, and relies on the handouts and good graces of our residents. Apparently, she got tired of dealing with the changing environment. Found it harder to keep doing eagle types of things, lost her sense of balance, and began to waste away. Let go of her once mighty presence as age set in and cares not to exert efforts to hunt, fish, or support herself. Ended up here in my tree."

Biter gazed up at the tattered brown and white creature. "She must have been a beauty in her day," she observed. Then she said goodbye and departed, her stumpy cattle dog tail wagging in the distance.

EPISODE 333 – UNCTIOUS

"I'M NOT GOING TO take this lying down like you guys," Rat Dog bellowed. "I'll squeal what she fed us to every dog everywhere. It's only then that we'll get action and I'll receive my proper Delights!"

"You will not," Dingo stated abruptly. "First, you're always lazily lying down, and seeing you do anything else would be quite a surprise. Second, please give us a minute to enjoy the refreshing sound of quiet from your wormy lips. Now, what does everyone else have to say about our visitor?"

Daisy's stump was vibrating. "She was nice and reminded me of me. Also, I'm not totally sure, but I believe she was up on the rocks with the Swatter Bowl Mangi."

"Seriously?" Dug wondered. "A Mangi trekking so far to visit measly old us? We're not that important. How did you arrive at this conclusion?"

"My nose. When at the Swatter Bowl, I was too far away to see their coats, especially since they were wearing the big neck cones. Besides, my eyes aren't great at distance, but I do recall her scent."

Dingo nodded in thought. "Well, if she was an actual Swatter Bowl Mangi, then she clearly took a risk in coming here. Assuming this news is true about certain of them taking Ponce pills and powders to live far longer, what can we do with that? Wail it aloud for all to hear, as the tick suggests? On the flip, we have no proof besides her hearsay account."

"Let's make a show of it, I insist. It's not as if they'll boot us from our houses if we raise a fuss. They've already done that," Rat Dog whined.

"Though they could still kick Dug and me out of our home," Bad-Boy complained.

"Yeah, we don't want that. At least you and Dug get to stay at our great old digs," Daisy observed.

Dug frowned, "But it's lonelier without you."

Crusty was meandering by them and rubbing up against each, except for Rat Dog. "Oh, seriously now! So few creative conniving capabilities you canines retain, but I may have a scheme to acquire the needed evidence."

"Really?" Dingo asked, wide-eyed.

"Yes. I know a friend of a friend of a friend who might be able to get access to the Mangi food and water containers. We could have him scrape off a bit of their dinner slop, then test for these longevity pills and powders. That kind of proof could convince many that certain Swatter Bowl Mangi are intending to rule and drool over us for forever, meaning very long. Besides, we cats have an ongoing gripe with The Caste and the entire favoritism, canine dominance system. We're perennially treated inferior to their high and mighty selves. Today, we have no voice in how things are run because they've stacked the decks against us through various edicts and issuances. Few of my kind hold any remaining hope for change."

Dingo was contemplating her plan. "Assuming we move ahead, we'd need to put our best noses on the case. Noses that could determine whether what's in the food bowls is the same as the pure stuff."

Daisy volunteered happily. "I possess one of the best noses in town!"

Crusty smiled. "And another friend of a friend of a friend will help us get the pure Ponce stuff to compare. Give us a paws-worth of days, then we should have confirmation as to whether they are or are not

DAISY THE DUMPSTER DOG - A SORDID TALE OF DYSTOPIAN HUBRIS AND CONVENIENT CANINE RATIONALIZATIONS

walking a path of effulgent, eternal rule over the effusively unruly and unhappy."

A few moons passed since their visit to Daisy and Dingo in Felinus, and BadBoy and Dug were back but barely surviving at the lair. One morning, BadBoy was awakened by an unusual clamor, though he was not about to get up to investigate.

"What's that noise?" BadBoy complained. "Can't sleeping dogs lie anymore?"

"It's definitely a commotion in motion," Dug observed from the lair's opening. "Mongrel hoards are peacefully treading past the dumpsters, and it appears they're headed in the general direction of the Swatter Bowl. I also see a few cats in the mix as well as coyotes and racnines, of all things."

BadBoy was feeling rotten and forgotten. Due to the bad blood between Daisy, Dingo, Rat Dog and the entire Caste and Mangi establishment, he and Dug were pushed a few rungs down the status ladder. Instead of waiting for Nemesys and gang to have first dibs before they could jump in for seconds or thirds, they were now slightly above where rats and crows stood, among the lowest of lows. That meant very little to eat in otherwise very big stomachs. His ungainly coat was beginning to slough-off in chunks, and Dug's slobbery mouth was drying up. These were bad signs, he knew. "I'm hungry enough to eat dirt," he whined.

"Shush!" Dug demanded. "You think you've lost weight? Look at me! Nothing remains but crinkly skin. An old friend asked if I was a Shar Pei. Big insult there. I'm starting to realize that I have a nose, and a strong breeze lifted me off my fours yesterday. If we could only go back in time and have things be the way they were. It wasn't perfect, but it was better."

BadBoy sighed. "The unctuous and unjust societal undulations just keep getting unjuster, and we're caught in the undertow. Perhaps one day The Caste and Swatter Bowl Mangi will forget about this unfortunate episode. Maybe they'll move on. But simply having been buddies with those rascals has placed us in the dreaded doghouse, probably for the rest of our miserable lives. If I had the energy and inclination, I'd have half a mind to join them permanently in Felinus right now. Don't have the strength to get there, though. Do you?"

Dug didn't respond. Instead, she was dumbfounded at what she saw coming her way. "Dingo?" she marveled.

And it was him. Dingo. He was striding toward her as if it was the old days. "Dug! Great to see you. Is BadBoy inside?"

"What are you doing?" she asked, both excited and frightened for a variety of reasons. "You understand there's a Swatter Bowl Mangi mandate to prevent dogbots from being near here? You're taking huge risks, and maybe we'll get collared again as a result, when we've suffered so harshly already. Few care about lowly canine suffering these days."

"Don't worry," he assured her. "They've asked me to come back. They shouldn't chain you up for that."

"Come back?" BadBoy's voice resounded from within the lair. "Does this mean our prior hierarchy status might be reinstated?"

"I doubt that," Dingo replied.

"Then I'll not get up to greet you, if you don't mind. Every movement has become a Herculean effort. I can only reserve my limited remaining energy to forage for scraps with the rats."

"Speaking of which," Dug wondered, "how are you and Daisy doing with that repulsive tick? You've spent multiple moons with him there, and he detests cats."

Dingo laughed. "I've learned to ignore his insults and baleful banter. But Daisy? She's not quite there yet, and the two constantly go at it. Yap yap yapping, all the time. But I haven't told you why I've been invited back here."

DAISY THE DUMPSTER DOG - A SORDID TALE OF DYSTOPIAN HUBRIS AND CONVENIENT CANINE RATIONALIZATIONS

"No, you haven't."

He smiled. "Have you noticed these protests going on?"

"I can't help but see them," she groaned. "It's been a daily parade of perritos and similar animals. What does that have to do with you?"

"The protests are having clear effect," he stated. "They always do. The Swatter Bowl Mangi are apparently concerned that they overstepped their bounds, that they're out of kilter with society overall, and that they should stop being so militantly dogmatic on their positions that favor the few and harm the many."

"And you put faith in this rumor?" she chuckled sadly.

"No," he said, shaking his head. "I don't trust these Demidog communers as far as I can chuck them, though that's pretty far. However, they asked me to appear before them at the Swatter Bowl and state a case for 'the lesser breeds,' as they put it. Considering the alternative, which is to let things get progressively worse, I thought I'd take them up on the offer."

Dug was dubious about the visit. "You don't actually believe they'd change anything, do you? That doesn't sound like the Swatter Bowl Mangi or Caste. These types have grown up their entire lives with Delights and benefits and entitlements that few are able to even dream about. Their 'I'm special and different' narratives are galvanized in their tiny furry tummies at birth. The fact that they said 'the lesser breeds' indicates how they think of us. You're barking up the wrong tree to confront them again, in my view."

Dingo smiled. "Indeed. Occasionally, they'll do something that either accidentally or overtly exposes their beastly biases. Yet, what's the alternative?"

"Probably more of these protests?" BadBoy growled from within the lair. "Given my bad luck lately, that's the certain outcome and I'll never sleep again. On second thought, if they dog-whistled for you to meet with them, maybe these protests are having a real effect. Again, I'd get up to go with you to the Bowl, but my legs are too weak from lack of chow."

"Are we allowed to attend," Dug wondered, "because I'll gladly go?"

"Nope. Sorry, girl. They're calling this a 'special session to make an impression.' Hope I'm not chasing my tail, though. Worst case, they'll use the opportunity to lash at me and prove how infused they are with the knowledge of their long-dead masters, meaning the ancient Demi-dogs. That all their prior edicts are meant to housetrain us for our own good. If so, at least I gave it my best shot."

Dug shook her head in doubt. "You're aware that the majority of them are tied at the hock to the Fidoish club or clique or cadre of conniving clandestine canines. I wish you good luck, but I'm not hopeful," she uttered, licking her dry lips.

EPISODE 334 – DEWORMED

DINGO PACED FORWARD BUT alone toward the Swatter Bowl. As he neared it, Nemesys sprinted toward him, with his gang trailing closely behind.

"You're not supposed to be here," Nemesys warned, sliding to a stop within a hair of Dingo. "Think you can take on my compadres now, dingbot? I doubt it, since you appear to be nursing a gimp leg. What happened there? A pack of racnines?"

Dingo smiled. "How'd you guess, buddy? Please, however, remove your hairy carcass from my path. I've been called to speak before the Swatter Bowl Mangi. If you mess with me, you're messing with them too."

"So we hear," Nemesys replied. "As much as I want to shred your metallic hide right here, my elevated Mangi contacts might find that unproductive. You, my friend, are about to be skewered by the best skewering pack of capable canines in dogdom. Hope you can pick up the pieces of your shattered self after this roasting. Wish I could be there to witness it. But I have ways of getting the inside poop afterward."

Nemesys and gang stepped aside as Dingo continued walking forward toward the Bowl. "Where's that mouthy creature you hang with? Miss that guy and Daisy, too. Give them our best regards, and I hope they've found a nice home among the odorous insects in Felinus," he joked sarcastically.

"Oh, we're doing fine," Dingo replied as he walked through the entry door of the Bowl.

Once inside, Dingo realized that it was only him. Him and the seven Mangi groomed in their usual cones and perched high on their respective rock overlooks.

"You're late," the Afghan observed. "No dogs arrive late to our proceedings. But then, you're not a real dog, are you?"

Dingo was about to respond politely to his oddly rude question, but the Afghan continued. "Can you comprehend why you've been placed before us?"

He was unsure how to answer since the question seemed somewhat condescending. "I wasn't placed, per se. I came here of my own volition, at your request, unless you know the truth to be otherwise."

"Don't talk to us about truth!" a regally coned Husky barked vociferously. "The truth is that you and your cohorts have been rabble-rousing and creating all kinds of trouble for us."

"And I did this from my exiled home in Felinus?" he wondered innocently.

"Multitudes of boorish beasts are spreading malicious rumors about us," the Afghan interjected. "We believe the ignoramus instigators are either you or that terrible rat terrier or Westie mix. Rumors about us using pills and powders to extend our lives. Doing unnatural things. Mocking us, even. This is utterly reprehensible to canines of our elevated stature. Unable to pinpoint the source at this moment, however, we'll move beyond these rumors to the issues at paw."

Dingo was entirely befuddled, thinking this was going to be what they implied it was in their invite: a potential for reconsideration of their prior positions. Not only about rescinding the ban on dogbots, chihuahuas, rat terriers, Westies, Westie mixes, and a few they had added to the onerous list since then. But also about the reason he appeared at the Swatter Bowl in the first place, which was to plead for them to moderate their dogma and doctrines a bit. To stop baying so loudly, to avoid overstretching their powers, and start behaving as if all canines mattered, not just their housetrained friends and family. But

DAISY THE DUMPSTER DOG - A SORDID TALE OF DYSTOPIAN HUBRIS AND CONVENIENT CANINE RATIONALIZATIONS

this hadn't gotten off on the right path, certainly not like he anticipated. He was trying to assess if he'd stepped in his own poop by being this naively forthright with them.

The Afghan continued to lead the dogalogue. "Can your limited intellect comprehend the pressure you've placed us under?"

"With regard to what, my friend?" Dingo replied meekly.

That was not the conscientious contrition the Afghan was seeking. "With regard; to the regard; in regard to; and regarding the lowbrow protests happening everywhere. Things were fine and finer before you showed up with your motley, mouthy rodent companion. We contemplated the issues brought before us, we communed with our beloved Demidog founders, and we issued edicts. It was so very disciplined and orderly. I'd almost say 'just and righteous.' Then you appeared."

"But that's not quite the case, sir, as I understand it," Dingo countered.

The Afghan was furious. "Not quite the case?" he repeated.

"No sir. As nearly every canine in dogdom knows, the majority of you at this Swatter Bowl have been bred at the pleasure of the Fidoish club or clique or cadre of conniving clandestine canines, and you fear falling out of favor with them and their trainers and benefactors. As a result, you often do what's right for them and their kind, but rarely do what's right for us innumerable lowly ones. Since they trained you and ingrained you, perhaps that makes sense. Can't teach an old dog new tricks, I guess. In addition, you apparently issue edicts by communing with the long-dead Demidogs and quoting the ancient and faultless wisdom of the Canistution. However, you appear to use that as convenient rationale only when it suits you and your self-assured, oft-regurgitated narratives to do so."

At this point, the Afghan and a few other Mangi were leaning forward and panting furiously. They were so perversely agitated and shaken that they were nearly tumbling from their high rock perches.

"I'm simply repeating what I've heard from numerous knowledgeable sources," Dingo continued, "and a bit of what I've observed myself. I have no reason to sit, lie down or roll over on this topic. And speaking of lying down, rumor is that you lie on your backs and scratch and wriggle in a bucolic, furballic frenzy while conjuring that communing thing. It's not my idea of a good roll in the grass, but whatever works for you is whatever works for you."

Totally engaged and utterly enraged, the Afghan lifted his palpitating paw high in the air and pointed menacingly at Dingo. "Not one more word," he howled as foam dripped profusely from his slack-jaw.

But Dingo was far from finished. "Perhaps it's simply embedded in your instinctual pedigree to sniff out a dead thing in the dirt, rub your nose in it, then grind that stale stench into your backside. In doing so, you can pretend to obtain the prescient and most holy vision of what that dead thing once was. So fun to pretend, isn't it? And how convenient for you to use this excuse to purify your conscience, convincing yourself that you are no slave to the salacious commands of your demadogue masters or snack-feeding benefactors. It's like finding that favorite spot in the yard to do all your dooty, then pretending your paws that prance there are as clean and pristine as a new dog whistle."

"I'll not be denigratingly tongue-lashed in my own house by a lowly dogbot or any canine anywhere," the Afghan bellowed. "Do you know who I am? Can you comprehend the perennial power that I wield?" He stopped for a second and thought better of his last comment. "That we Swatter Bowl Mangi wield?"

Having no fear built into his code, Dingo was only moderately perturbed by this canine's threats and rants, so he persisted. "Indeed, your power is quite impressive. I'm guessing you possess a crystal bowl to precisely comprehend why the Demidogs made the decisions they did. Imagine that: using a crystal bowl to transcend time and space and walk and wake in their precious pawprints and mindprints! Given your ability to conjure such special magic, can you just tell me one simple thing?

DAISY THE DUMPSTER DOG - A SORDID TALE OF DYSTOPIAN HUBRIS AND CONVENIENT CANINE RATIONALIZATIONS

When you next commune with those most brilliant among bowsers, please ask them why they gifted the Swatter Bowl Mangi with lifetime jobs."

At this point, Dingo was pretty parched and politely paused for questions or comments. "Are we close to where you were hoping to go with this conversation? You haven't spoken much."

The Afghan was not about to let this last assault go unanswered. "And how do you rate to wail and cry about our everlasting guarantees and protections of perennial power and presence? We exalted, vaulted Swatter Bowl Mangi were granted such brazenly bountiful and bodacious boons long ago by our founders, countless moons before you were ever mistakenly manufactured, so we're never dropping the ball on them. Indeed, indeed. Ever our reign shall be. So it be barked. So it be done."

"Well, let's just wait a minute, doggone it!" Dingo rebutted. "I've got a great idea. Why don't you go perform your magical, mystical communing with those same Demidogs who created that holy and infallible Canistution, and ask them yourselves about what they intended in this regard? No doubt they'll say they also possessed a crystal bowl like yours, but one that allowed them to perfectly envision our future. They'll claim they knew that you'd naturally live far longer than the malnourished and mistreated canines lived back in their days, due to anticipated advances in medical science and better quality kibble. And to top that off, they will have presciently predicted Ponce pills and powders to let you preach your perennial philosophies perennially. Yep, some old Demidog peered into that crystal bowl and barked, 'Myriad moons from now, the most high Swatter Bowl Mangi will endure innumerable dog days and will likely be faultless. Thusly, let's grant them eternal and everlasting jobs of power and prestige.'"

"Crystal bowl, my tail!" the Afghan whined.

"But wait again!" Dingo added. "Would it be fair and just if you, the most divine Swatter Bowl Mangi, were also the anointed ones to confirm these facts by communing with our dearly dead beloveds? Would it be fair if they informed you that they anticipated the day when dogs would live far longer, eventually to infinity, despite the fact no such science was even perceived possible at that time? Talk about uncanny clairvoyance!"

The Afghan frowned and snarled, "And why would this not be fair?"

Dingo smiled. "Well, isn't it obvious? You presently perch your paunches on these same palpable pedestals. You therefore can't be counted as neutral arbiters of decisions in which your lives and livelihoods and living histories and life stories are so intertwined that you might unintentionally bias the original interpretations of our deceased and decaying Demidogs. Any competent canine would agree with that most obvious conflict of interest. In fact, to attain puritanical clarity on this matter, you must concede such communing responsibilities on this topic to canines who have no paws in the game. I'm sure we could easily corral packs of mongrels to accept that weighty mantle. Then they can, like you, squiggle and squaggle their backsides in the grass and dirt for as long as required. Only then will the original visions of the founders be illuminated on this longevity topic, to be barked far and wide for all to appreciate and reverently, solemnly, and blindly follow."

The Husky stepped in because the Afghan was so infuriated at Dingo's immutable logic that he couldn't evoke another thought. "You've really messed up, buddy," the Husky warned. "Before you opened your mealy metallic mouth, we were considering whether or not to reconsider our earlier considerations. Yet, you've demonstrated that you are an entirely inconsiderate and inconsolable ingrate. So much for an attempt at being magnificently magnanimous on our part. Of course, we are slightly concerned about the state of the lowbrow dogs and what's got them downright riled up; not so much the cats or other animals, though. But your perfidious performance here proves that you and your menial ilk are incapable of elevating your tiny minds to our level for even the slightest moment, to contemplate the contemporary conditions and condescensions with which we must contend contemporaneously. I thereby command to you to scat and scram from here. Vamoose and away with you, annoying and insignificant pester-bot. If it was within my powers to do so, I'd forcibly have your entire body virus checked and dewormed, but perhaps there will be another occasion for that."

As the Husky finished her harangue, she motioned her paw forward in a sign for Dingo to shoo from the Swatter Bowl and pronto.

Acutely aware of the hostility they were showing him, he quickly darted out of there with his tail between his legs. That was a hard thing for a Basenji dogbot to do, but he managed.

On the return home, Dingo wasn't sure whether he should hang his head low because of his second Swatter Bowl failure, or raise his snout high because his visit was casually a success, in an odd way. However, he was certain of one thing: the canines in dogdom were experiencing a gradual, imperceptible, and dangerous degradation of their social structure, something the Demidogs could never have anticipated for the times in which they lived, which was a very long time ago.

EPISODE 335 – SPICY

UPON DINGO'S ARRIVAL AT home, their makeshift lair in Felinus, Daisy started pogoing as usual.

"How did it go, buddy?" she asked. "Did you convince them? I'm sure you did because you're so smart."

Rat Dog was making an effort to rise on his haunches, readying himself for a return to their old digs and Delights that evening. He was tiring of the same smelly fish bones and rancid meat, and he cared nothing for the field mice and half-dead rodents the cats brought into town. As a result of that poor diet, he was actually losing lardage.

"What took you?" he complained, frowning angrily at Dingo. "My stomach's been waiting. Now that we're fully reinstated, I'm standing right there this afternoon, right in front of Nemesys and his lackeys. They can try to jostle their way in front of me to get first dibs at Delights, but I'm a vicious and viscous but wily speed demon when I need to be."

Staring at his friends, he wasn't sure how to impart the bad news. "Well," Dingo began, "I showed up on time, though the Afghan said I wasn't. I guess he's the alpha dog among them. Despite how it appeared from the outset, despite how hopeful we were that they would reconsider, such a thing was not in their plans from the start. Unfortunately, the majority were present to give me a good old dog whipping."

"Ugh!" Rat Dog groaned. "You failed to take the cake again, much less bring us any?"

"Tell us," Daisy urged, her excitement finally tempered.

DAISY THE DUMPSTER DOG - A SORDID TALE OF DYSTOPIAN HUBRIS AND CONVENIENT CANINE RATIONALIZATIONS

"Tough to say. I was running in circles. They'd ask a question, I'd respond truthfully, and the Afghan or that Husky would tear into me like meat on a bone. When I tried to behave respectfully, it seemed I was digging a bigger hole for myself. I couldn't help but be truthful since it's not within me to lie or feign reverence or pretend piety to any canine at any point or occasion. We are all just dogs in this world. Politeness, sure. Reverence, no."

"You opened your mouth to squeal in that demented dogbot way, and I don't get to eat for a year," Rat Dog cried, utterly fraught with frustration as the reality was beginning to hit him. "I should've gone instead of you. I clearly would have cooked up a far better performance. Besides, I never froze before them as if I was a newborn pup, and they already had a clear indication that I was their intellectual equal."

Dingo's head shook dejectedly. "This was never about being equals with them. They have the power and claim the Swatter Bowl as their marked territory. You don't win there; you only come away shamed and derided, I guess, unless you are friends of friends or you espouse the dogma of the Fidoish club or clique or cadre of conniving clandestine canines. This was not going to be about their contrition, apparently. It was intended to be about mine on behalf of us lonely and lowly slogs and dogs. Perhaps it would have gone better had I nodded obediently with my head bowed, begging at the table of shame and heeling, rolling over, and sitting at their command."

"We're toast!" Rat Dog lamented. "Emaciated, rotting canine toast. Notice that? Everything I talk about now is a reference to food."

Ever the optimist, Daisy tried to console her friend. "Dingo, there are things we can't change in the world. Such haughty pooches will always be with us. They're bred from pups to believe they're smarter or purer or raised in a superior way. Then their coercive, corrosive and clannish little packs and dens reinforce that narrative along the well-designed paths they tread. So, they can't help themselves from feeling and acting and thinking entitled. It's encoded in their genetic lineages and perfidious pedigrees. Alphas, betas, omegas and similar words which I rarely use. Some canines really go for those superiority and dominance narratives. I've seen it in the way they laugh teasingly at my bobbed tail or loveable and majorly outstanding ears."

"Bread from pups? Wish I had some of that now. Please don't bark another word about food," Rat Dog lamented.

Suddenly, Crusty jumped up from behind the tree and into her usual spot on the branch, her front paw hanging low to whack at the occasional fly, of which there were many about the place. "Why the glums, my chums?" she wondered.

"Our famed circus dog gave his second cupcake performance at the Swatter Bowl today, along with the dancing bears and monkey playing an accordion," Rat Dog groaned. "They didn't even throw him a bone or a dessicated, worm-infested yard cigar to chew on. As expected, he lived up to his legend, meaning circus boy failed to convince our illustrious Mangi most high to allow us to come back and once again participate in delectable Delights. So, Crusty, for the rest of my days I get to experience the pleasure of lovely Ammoniaville searing my nostrils, as well as an astounding array of glutinous goodies you guys catch. Freshly mangled mice, for example, with a toothpick's worth of meat left on them. The occasional dead buzzard that expired from a deadly, transmittable disease and has been baking in the sun. Woe to the dogtrodden such as me, for they are the lowest of lows who are troddened to dust."

Crusty stared at him in disbelief. She knew that some dogs could be jaundiced at times, but was surprised that this one dog could be jaundiced all the time. For his part, Dingo was so dejected that he had no retort.

"Sorry to hear that," she said, "but I came with good news, friends. We received a confirmation. Daisy, you're already aware since you participated. Do you want to tell them?"

DAISY THE DUMPSTER DOG - A SORDID TALE OF DYSTOPIAN HUBRIS AND CONVENIENT CANINE RATIONALIZATIONS

Daisy hadn't put two and two together on this. She knew that Dingo got swatted at the Swatter Bowl, true to form. She also recalled that she had participated in their previously planned sniff test. But she lacked the walnut girth to make the connection between the two events.

"Sure!" she yelped happily. "Along with a few paws full of similarly talented noses, I smelled the smells from the bowls and from Crusty's friends. We arrived at the same conclusion."

She then stopped mid-air, recalling how fine and fantastic the food smelled. "I'd love to find the canine chef who's preparing the Mangis' bowls. They have the most excellent food I've ever tasted. Real first-class stuff. You'd think they'd have gained considerable poundage with that cooking. There were spices I never knew existed..."

Luckily, Dingo stopped her. "Daisy! You're off on a tangent and failed to tell us what was discovered."

"Huh?" she questioned. "I told you already. I found the greatest smells and hope someday to sniff more of them up close, possibly in my own bowl."

Dingo dazed hopelessly up at Crusty and shrugged his shoulders. "Is there new news here, or is this only about the spices?"

Crusty nodded and smiled wryly. "The news is pretty spicy, indeed. Each of the testers concluded the same thing: a paw's full of Mangi, including the dewclaw, had significant amounts of the anti-aging Ponce pills and powders in their bowls. In fact, we think that's the reason their food is so heavily spiced. The Ponce stuff doesn't taste good on its own, and they are forced to douse it with additional strong flavors and aromas. On occasion, I have to do the same with rancid rats."

Rat Dog, who was standing up while listening to Daisy and Crusty drone on, immediately fell to the ground and started shaking as if he had accidentally just sat on a fire ant hill.

"Rattie!" Daisy howled. "Are you dying? Did a snake bite you? I don't see a snake, and I don't even get what purpose they serve, though I never knew one personally."

"Daisy!" Dingo barked again, hoping to shut her up. "It might be the heebie-jeebies or perhaps he's having psychotic visions that he's rolling in poop. Consider that he's gone a few days without real food, which could explain this delirium. Let's give him a second to see if he snaps out of it."

But lack of food wasn't it, although it was indirectly it. Psychotic visions of foisting about in poop wasn't it, either. Nor was it the heebie-jeebies, though his dark resolve might have led some to think so. It was, instead, a vision of unique genius, which arose rarely in a normal dog's life.

Finally, Rat Dog stopped thrashing in the dirt beneath the tree and sat up straight, his now ragged and broken leg cast showing the worse for wear. "I have the answer," he proclaimed, "the answer to my troubles. The path to rightful righteousness. A vision so profound that I'll be known as the savior to the dogtrodden canines, even including felines who are the lowest of lows."

Crusty hissed at that remark. "Hey, you're standing on my ground, dude. Besides, you eat the rats I catch for you."

"Shush!" he commanded. "Take offense if you will. Jump a fence if you want. Play defense, if that suits you." Then he stopped midstream. His eyes began bugging out, and he started backwards sneezing. "Whee-ung. Whee-ung. Whee-ung!"

They were pretty used to seeing that behavior in canines and the occasional cat, but never in Rat Dog.

Daisy was worried. "He's dying!" she cried. "See his eyes? They're totally bloodshot and his face looks terrible. He can't breathe! Imagine that, expiring dramatically before he can voice his astounding idea! Sadly, he'll never get to tell us about his righteous path."

DAISY THE DUMPSTER DOG - A SORDID TALE OF DYSTOPIAN HUBRIS AND CONVENIENT CANINE RATIONALIZATIONS

"He won't die," Dingo replied, disgusted in his performance. "I'm guessing he wasn't getting enough attention because we weren't talking about him. He's faking a backwards sneeze because he really has no profound vision. It's a false flag intended to lure our short-term minds to his meaningless mental mishap of the moment."

"False flag? My butt!" Rat Dog hacked as he was coming out of it. "That reaction was as real as Daisy's nubbed tail."

"Then what is this brain fart you claimed would change the nature of our worlds? We haven't forgotten," Crusty inquired.

"I'll tattle," he whimpered in response.

"What's that again?" Crusty asked.

"I'll tattle," he coughed. "I'll get the word out so that every animal under their jurisdiction will hear the truth."

"Regarding what?" Daisy wondered. "That you faked a backward sneeze?"

Dingo was having none of it. "No, it doesn't mean that. It means he'll let the world know what we just confirmed: that the Swatter Bowl Mangi are taking Ponce pills and powders to extend their lives forever. I'll remind you that they were gifted lifetime jobs by the Canistution and its archaic Demidog founders. So long, in fact, that the Demidogs never would have foreseen that such science might exist. Do you really think they'd have granted lifetime jobs to canines if the doggone pooches were to live and rule for such extended periods, even to forever?"

He stopped for a moment to see if this was making sense to any of them. It wasn't, so he continued. "Of course not! It's one of the most obvious and egregious instances where the Demidog founders created the Canistution very long ago, and things have changed considerably since then. However, we still expect the Canistution to be resolutely and exactly interpreted as if we were still living in those days. That was innumerable moons before canines were even capable of reaching the extended ages we do today, even without magical pills and powders.

Why, a dog currently lives two or three times the length of time versus back then, and the Demidogs certainly didn't factor that into their fortuitous, gratuitous lifetime grants."

He stopped again for the same reason and only saw glazed eyes. So he persisted. "To imagine: our illustrious founders were so worried about Swatter Bowl Mangi being corrupted by the powerful who might employ them after they left their positions, that they instead granted them lifetime jobs. And what is the result in these heady days? We have Swatter Bowl Mangi who, even when unaided by longevity pills and powders, live and rule and issue edicts far longer than the Demidogs ever could have anticipated. Yet there's more! They'll now live forever, rule forever, and be societal top dogs forever due to advanced science like these Ponce pills and powders. I may have mentioned this concern previously, but it's okay if I repeat it. The whole situation is sucky. Sucky's the day. Sucky's the night. Sucky means eternity."

At least Rat Dog was understanding some of Dingo's diatribe. "And since they often rule against the lowly and dogtrodden, we will forever be the lowly and dogtrodden. This is why my plan is so deviously brilliant!" he exclaimed.

"Devious? Yes. Brilliant? No," Dingo countered. "Who will care if you tattle tale this to any beast with a tail?"

"Hey!" Daisy interjected.

"Or without a tail," Dingo added. "You recall what happened when the canines started protesting their recent decisions? Nothing. The Swatter Bowl Mangi are untouchable. They're the big fish. The top bananas. The steaming enchiladas, all wrapped and warped up in a big, fried tortilla."

Rat Dog pleaded, "Shut it with the food references, already!"

"But you get my drift, right?" Dingo proceeded. "Such impotent and insolent protests are only seen as detestable in those vaulted and exalted Mangi eyes. Detestable and slightly embarrassing, but otherwise harmless. They could care less what lowly bowsers think since they

DAISY THE DUMPSTER DOG - A SORDID TALE OF DYSTOPIAN HUBRIS AND CONVENIENT CANINE RATIONALIZATIONS

prance and dance around all day in some dreamy, delectable, Epicurean dimension of a dog's life. Their world is one of being the big cheeses at parties with Delights and heavily spiced food and all they can drink, while wearing cool neck cones like ice cream dandies."

"I said to stop it with the food references!" Rat Dog demanded. "The problem with you, dingbot, is that you don't dream big. I'm not talking just a few of us. I can imagine large hordes of adherents to my story. I can envision dust clouds that choke the air from the relentless and plentiful prances of paws on dirt."

Dingo was still having none of it. "You think you can get that kind of participation by simply tattling that they're using longevity pills and powders? No way. We've been bred to be docile and friendly. We tolerate pain and suffering and lack of food and water, then go whimper in a closet or doghouse by our lonesomes after being further abused. That's the lot in life for us and cats, I daresay. Constant abuse and misuse, coupled with intolerable tolerance on our part. Likely a hopeful whimper or wagging tail after the fact, excusing dogs without tails, Daisy. I think we could sleep right through a tornado and not lift our heads from the ground as it twists away our shelters, families, and livelihoods. It's a confusing infusion of acceptance about our lowly role. That's what I'm saying. Spilling this revelation out to the world is no different than sniffing butts. Sniff one, and you've sniffed them all. Nothing exciting here. Turn your butt cheek when swatted and carry on. To conclude, we societal runts of the litter who fail to take action should and will get what's coming to us, and it's not Delights."

Unfazed by such discouraging words from the normally sanguine Dingo, Rat Dog jabbered out his plan. "What you said may be true, but many canines will finally get off their haunches and move when collar-shocked, and this serves as the shock. I'll tell them the Mangi are using Ponce pills and powders so that they might dominate, regulate, administer, mandate, and rule the slate against us from this moment until time's end. That means these same illustrious, resplendent few would rule not only them, but their pups, their pups' pups, and on down the canine line of repression. When I've riled, wrestled, and wrangled enough of these doggies, I'll lead them in peaceful marches directly to the Swatter Bowl. We'll protest there relentlessly. Look at me! I'm already effectively on a hunger strike because I no longer have access to Delights. What do a few more days without food matter to me? You see, I'm no different than a goose's gaggle of four-legged creatures who are suffering the same fate: Delights are designated for The Caste and precious friends and benefactors, all of whom are among the favored. The rest of us are forced to share the bitter bites at the bottom of the barrel. This cannot and will not go on forever!"

EPISODE 336 – LEAP

FOR ONCE, RAT DOG did what he said he would do, and actually followed through on his words. He had Dingo smash his cast that day so that he could gimp around dogdom's territories more effectively. With anger and hunger and an undying sense of fairness driving his limited but singularly focused psyche, he personally hobbled to visit the dogtrodden in adjacent lands. At every location, he spilled the full can of beans for them to lap up. He excelled at painting the sordid picture of how the bones were stacked against them for the sole benefit of the fatty ham hocks at the top, doing his best to expose the unseen, unforeseen, and serpentine ways that Swatter Bowl Mangi decisions so doggedly advantaged the hocks and adversely affected the everyday lives of the lowly.

He would often begin his barking remarks by yelping something similar to this: "If each one of you continues to sit on your fat arses; if all you care to do is lie like a dog the whole day long, whining and whimpering; if you prefer to squeal at the top of your lungs, hoping another canine will take heart and relieve you of your heavy collars; if you'd rather chase your tails than tell the tales of courage that you might have lived; and if you act like a dead dog, then you'll become a dead dog for society's sake."

"Gaze upon me for inspiration!" he'd bawl. "A shattered front leg and starving belly. Few friends that speak highly of me. Cat calls from the multitudes that oppose my views. I don't do this for fun, you animals. I do this because I have the guts to change my situation; to protest where I must protest; to influence change and create fairness at all levels of our society; and ultimately, to take action, not to fake action."

Given the chub's influence and ability to stir a crowd, action is indeed what his listeners, admirers, and advocates took. Dens upon litters upon packs upon kennels upon clutters and clusters of canines, felines, and other four-leggers protested openly on any pathway, as Rat Dog continued whipping up a furred frenzy of fury.

Over the countless moons of his travels, he thought he almost died on multiple occasions due to disenfranchised racnine and coyote verbal attacks, as well as canines and cats who just didn't take well to his personality or looks. Again, he thought he almost died in these situations, but he didn't. Daisy, Dingo, Blister, and his other friends frequently accompanied him, except when they needed relief from his incessant complaining, which was often.

Multiple moons later, after many conniption fits, scuffles, tussles, and tumbles in dogdom, the crew agreed to meet in Felinus under the tree.

"Rat Dog, you old coot!" Daisy howled as she approached her old friend. Before reaching him, she had to turn and bite incessantly at her zinging hindquarter injury, the one she had suffered in the infamous racnine confrontation. She attempted to jump high into the air, but both the injury and hip dysplasia dampened her enthusiasm, so she licked his cheek instead.

"Even with these cataracts, I could still see your ears bouncing annoyingly from a long distance away," Rat Dog chided. "Did you ever get yourself checked? I mean, I seriously doubt you're a true canine. Given that I've known you all these moons, the rumors about you being a genetic mishap or off-target reject are likely true."

"Thanks for the compliment, old friend," she said, wagging what nominal stub remained on her hind end. "I never did find my tail, though I searched for it. One must conclude that it's still in that cold

DAISY THE DUMPSTER DOG - A SORDID TALE OF DYSTOPIAN HUBRIS AND CONVENIENT CANINE RATIONALIZATIONS

box. I'm sure the white coat standies regularly take it out to create clones. I mean, who wouldn't want to be happy old me?"

"Still getting along with your standies, then?" he inquired. "I can't believe you ever located them. That must've taken intense searching. Dumb luck, more likely."

"Ah, Rat Dog," she relayed, "you know this famous nose. I kept sniffing and eventually caught their scent. But they remain my best standies family and always play with my toys, except when they're ignoring me. And once in a while, they discover where I did a dooty when they weren't around, then I dash into the small box where my bed is to hide. How about you?"

Rat Dog grimaced. "No standie ever picked me up, nor did I want to be. Never preferred a standie I ever met, and none were willing to tolerate my constant nipping at them. Those were only wake-up calls and not real chomps. Little did they care that I still experience lingering pain from my shattered ribs and contusions from that historical leap I made from fifty boxes up. And the first thing the standies want to do is grab at you. So, what am I supposed to do? Just let the wiseacres crush my barely healed bones? No. I bite. Hard. Nonstop and with ardent fervor. And it hurts. Who'd want these fangs slipping into their hides?"

He bared his few remaining teeth, and she laughed. "Not me. You always were the toughest of all, including Dingo. Hey, here he comes now!"

"Where? I don't see him."

"That's because your eyes are half-cataracts," she countered.

"No different from yours," he replied. "Then again, you never much needed your eyes given the unnatural antenna they genetically manufactured for your head. I'd hate to have gone through life with donkey ears like that. Constant headaches from muscle spasms, trying to keep them lifted upright."

"And what of our catty friend?" Daisy wondered.

"Hello there," Crusty purred from above. "Good to see you again, my dear, though I do believe they should be termed 'dogaracts' instead since you canines seem to get those eye afflictions more often than us cats."

She gazed upward at her graying tabby buddy. "I'm wagging, Crusty, but this stubby stump doesn't work as well, nor do these hips. That springing up and down at everything, I suppose. Worn to the bone. Appears you and Rattie made a nice home for yourselves here."

"Not by choice," he interjected, "but luckily my nostrils finally burned to a crisp. Death from ammonia. And not having a sense of smell or taste, food simply became less important to me. In a twist of fate, it became a blessing of sorts."

"How's that?" Daisy wondered.

"No taste meant less food which meant lower weight which means I can still walk on my fours, despite the splintered front leg that never healed properly because of all the walking you guys made me do."

"That's dubious," Crusty added. "I'm forced to go hunt at night and bring back a thin mouse or other forlorn creature. And me, a vegetarian, doing all this for him for so long now."

Daisy noticed the lack of a lizard tail twitching in her mouth. "And what of your smaller reptilian buddies and displays of discipline?"

Crusty jumped from her branch and rubbed her side against Daisy's back. "At my age, I have nothing left to prove to the world. Besides, they tickled my tongue, and on more than one occasion, I was very tempted to chomp down."

The other three were now nearing the tree.

"Dingo. Dug. BadBoy!" Daisy yelped, running up to them. "Super glad to see you again."

Then she noticed Dingo carrying a leash in his mouth, which was attached to BadBoy's collar. "What's going on?" she wondered.

"Aye yai yai!" Dingo responded. "The old boy falls asleep regularly, even on short treks. He requested the collar-leash thing for me to jolt

DAISY THE DUMPSTER DOG - A SORDID TALE OF DYSTOPIAN HUBRIS AND CONVENIENT CANINE RATIONALIZATIONS

him awake when he fades, and I had to do that too many times on this jaunt."

"He still reeks as if he's never had a bath," Rat Dog groaned. "Thankfully, we're out here in the open and my sniffer is frosted, otherwise I'd be gagging chunks, or is it 'chunking gags?'"

Few things had changed for BadBoy, beyond a more regular diet of Delights. "Well," he said, his head hanging low, "I was about to go out one day when water dropped from on high. Lots of it. But I was sleepy and couldn't muster the gumption."

"And 'must' or 'musty' are appropriate words, in your case," Rat Dog joked.

As expected, Dug felt she was not getting enough attention. "Anyone going to yip at me? Crusty? Daisy? Heck, I'd even take a verbal slight from Rat Dog."

"Oh, Dug, I'm sorry. It was odd to see Dingo leading BadBoy with that leash. How are you?" Daisy wanted to lick her face but was kind of grossed out by the saliva slop slowly dripping off her jowls.

"Generally okay, though my allergies are acting up and that's exacerbating this slobberfest. I always placed last in every conversation, given my need to constantly slurp up this stuff."

Rat Dog sniveled, "No, it's because nobody can tell which end you're speaking from. They get confused, as I still am. You can't help your inferior breeding, I suppose."

Dug shook her head in disgust. "Crusty, how could you possibly tolerate spending time with this tick? I'm surprised you or your friends haven't popped him one. But then, he continues to feign that leg injury, so I can understand."

Crusty had rubbed her side against everyone, and was now on her back, swatting at BadBoy's dusty dreadlocks that hung nearly to the ground. "It's part of my self-discipline routine, still in effect. If I can stand being around this guy, then I can handle anything."

"And speaking of tolerance," Dingo said, "that's kind of why I wanted to get us together in one spot."

"Really?" Daisy asked. "I thought you only wanted to see our smiling faces."

He sighed. "Yes, that too. But I meant to say how proud I am of us."

Daisy was ecstatic. "I am, too. I mean, we look pretty good for our ages. That's something to be proud about."

Dingo expected her to provide that flippant commentary, so he continued. "If it wasn't for us digging up painful bones, scooping the poop, and marking our territories, things might be different today. We'd probably still have that crazy old process of giving Swatter Bowl Mangi non-rotating jobs with certain ones living eternal lifetimes from Ponce pills and powders. Added to that, we might have The Caste and Fidoish club or clique or cadre of conniving clandestine canines running rabid and rampant, doing their darndest and dankest to favor the already favored, no doubt backed by the surreptitious and sneaky Caociphus and GogMadDog, whoever or whatever they are. However, they remain alive and kicking and are as predictable in their plotting as periodical cicadas. So, I'd say we did a pretty good job of things and should be proud of our canine and feline selves."

"Cicadas?" Daisy cried. "They're my favorite crunchy food!"

"How wrong!" Rat Dog howled. "You forgot the part about where you were supposed to speak at your Swatter Bowl appearance, then got humiliated by a bout of ill-timed stage fright. Where I was forced to take immediate action and stand before innumerable crowds, a lonesome yet unswerving dove, and plead my case. You forgot how impressive I was when barking before them; how they agreed to my demands; how the pups and kittens took to me; how I traveled the lands to rile and wrangle the crowds into action; and how I became the heroic hero of antiheroes and unanticipated gyros."

"Gyros?" Dug wondered. "Sorry, brainchild, but gyros are sandwiches occasionally included in the Delights bags."

DAISY THE DUMPSTER DOG - A SORDID TALE OF DYSTOPIAN HUBRIS AND CONVENIENT CANINE RATIONALIZATIONS

"Hey, don't interrupt," he demanded. "I'm old and can make a few mistakes. Either way, you get where I was going. Without me, you'd all be dust, withering away from lack of food and buffeted by the wind and rains, with the exception of BadBoy, of course."

"Indeed," BadBoy admitted.

"Well," Daisy concluded. "I may not know a lot, but I do know that I like you guys and miss you completely, solemnly, and resolutely. I miss the old times with you, and I even miss Rat Dog's constant complaining and claims about his now infamous leap. By the way, can you once again remind us how many flaming boxes you leapt from?"

Rat Dog looked sheepish and knew, at least with this crowd, that it might be best to tone it down for once. "At least two," he admitted.

EPISODE 337 – TEDIUMDUM

ONE OF THE MOST impressive societal advancements that Rat Dog helped bring to dogdom was in regard to certain norms and entitlements, which were commonly thought of as the gospel truth as defined and codified by the beloved Demidogs. But in reality, they were neither the gospel nor the truth. More importantly, none of them were very well-delineated or well-defined anywhere, though some who held the power at the time had hoped this fact would not be checked.

Many norms and entitlements were only a result of 'longstanding interpretations' of the Demidogs' vague and imprecise words and wishes. Indeed, their hallowed howls regularly suffered from immense fallibility and inexactness, making them subject to slicing, dicing, and splicing of potential meanings and intentions. And Rat Dog exposed multiple examples of this as relates to the Swatter Bowl.

Firstly, Rat Dog identified that an exact number of Swatter Bowl Mangi was never specifically specified as a specification in the Canistution. Indeed, the current number was so small that it begged at the table to be usurped, burped, and biased in favor of a few immoderate and radical caninical viewpoints, especially given the poorly considered, luck-of-the-draw process for selecting these vaulted and exalted Mangi.

Dogdom's best dogisticians were thusly employed to find a way to make the most high body less likely to be corrupted by clubs or cliques and such. After intensive gnashing of teeth and dogged devotion to the Caninus Limit Theorem, the discerning dogisticians determined that six paws' full, including the dewclaw, was the optimal quantity of Swat-

DAISY THE DUMPSTER DOG - A SORDID TALE OF DYSTOPIAN HUBRIS AND CONVENIENT CANINE RATIONALIZATIONS

ter Bowl Mangi. But why? Because six paws' full mathematically guaranteed a far more equitable, balanced, and representative cross-section of the beliefs and values and morays and eels of canine society. Not perfect, but good enough. Besides, they would have run out of rock pedestals had they picked a larger number.

Secondly, and interestingly enough, Rat Dog pointed out that nothing in the Canistution ever definitively defined that the most high and exalted Swatter Bowl Mangi, or any Mangi for that matter, must absolutely and forever retain, maintain, and sustain the exact same posts to which they were first leashed.

As Rat Dog was wont to argue: "The most holy Canistution only provided that Mangi should 'hold their offices if they behave like good dogs.' In other words," he would spout, "if the Demidogs had meant to speak otherwise, they would have simply, clearly, indisputably and indefatigably barked as such: 'All Mangi shall forever and till the end of dog days keep and secure the exact same positions, titles, and Bowls to which they were originally assigned, and never be allowed to change or give them up, assuming they behave, of course.' But they didn't."

Since the Demidogs failed to decidedly, absolutely, and resolutely yap it this way, their original intentions would always be subject to 'interpretation, intonation, and infestation' of the interpreter. Notably, and as an indisputable fact, many Mangi had willfully shifted between Bowls in prior times, whether over, under, sideways, or down. Also up. Therefore, consistently 'cycling' them between the various Bowls appeared to be the foremost solution for most every situation.

Not surprisingly, this monumental change to longstanding norms was initially opposed by many most high Mangi who objected in principle and didn't want to learn how to cycle. Their objections, however, were eventually and inelegantly resolved. Basically, it got back to what Dingo suggested during his second embarrassing performance at the Swatter Bowl about communing with the Demidogs to determine their original and most divine intentions.

All agreed that the Swatter Bowl Mangi could not do the communing on this topic themselves due to conspicuous conflicts of interest. The objectionable Swatter Bowl Mangi were therefore given an option to train a gaggle of lowly dogs about how to commune. Once trained, those lowly dogs could transcendently relate exactly, specifically, and holistically what the Demidogs meant by the barked phrase 'Mangi shall hold their offices.'

For whatever obviously unobvious reasons, those argumentative Swatter Bowl Mangi suddenly backed off when presented with this option, then conceded to the cycling. That was a hard thing for the black-coned, four-legged doggies to do, but they did it in the name of good canine relations. Also, because protesting wails from the multitudes of unhappy lowly dogs got so loud and obnoxious that they were finding it hard to sleep.

Once all the old biases and customs regarding this particular 'hold their offices' topic were shed like a bad winter coat, a regular cycling of Mangi indeed occurred across the lands. They'd spend some of their time among the many local Bowls, a little less in the fewer intermediate Bowls, and even more less in the most high Swatter Bowl.

Thirdly was the other issue of what 'hold their offices' implied in terms of time in office, since 'lifetime' was never specifically referenced by the revered founders and the word 'hold' was about as vague as any dog could imagine. Most hounds had heard of the 'halt' command, and a few perceptive ones knew what it meant, but few understood 'hold.'

Some interpreted 'hold' as meaning a dog's normal lifetime of work, which was not all that many seasons, but one that would allow for a well-deserved retirement. Others assumed it meant a typical physical lifetime for a dog, which included even more seasons, all the way until their snouts turned gray or they expired the day. Still others insisted it as meaning 'forever and ever, including all the way to the dissolution of the universe into its final state of entropy,' should the canine live that long.

DAISY THE DUMPSTER DOG - A SORDID TALE OF DYSTOPIAN HUBRIS AND CONVENIENT CANINE RATIONALIZATIONS

It was imperfectly clear that such interpretations were subject to interpretations by the subject, and therefore relatively nonsensical. To make matters worse, premium kibble and white coat standies' care of the present-day canines allowed them to thrive far longer than back in the Demidogs' days. To make matters even worse, as Dingo and Rat Dog both pointed out, it was pretty improbable that the founders would have predicted Ponce pills and powders that might indeed allow eternally gifted canines to experience that final, universal entropic state.

Given the doggone mess of interpretations once considered as gospel, all of dogdom agreed that the Swatter Bowl Mangi could not fairly litigate this particular 'hold' issue due to manifest interest conflicts. Once again, the Mangi were offered the option to train lowly dogs to commune with the founders. When done, they could then determine whether the Demidogs indeed had a crystal bowl that gave them the wherewithal and werewolfall to foresee such life-extending science. And finally, once again, those certain objectionable most high Mangi decided to back-off in favor of a more equitable solution.

That equitable solution was simply this: Swatter Bowl Mangi were now being regularly cycled anyway, and because many more of them existed as working dogs, there was less of a chance of the august body becoming immutably imbalanced. To settle the 'hold to eternity' issue, it was determined that any Mangi who partook in Ponce pills and powders or similar longevity treatments would be limited to a number of seasons in their job equal to the quantity of Swatter Bowl Mangi. Assuming they didn't partake, then they would end up kicking the bowl naturally at some point, and that would be that.

With these thorny issues in the paws finally resolved, society improved a lot for the lowly and multitudinous multitudes. But whatever happened to the Fidoish club or clique or cadre of conniving clandestine canines, Caociphus, and GogMadDog – whoever they were, and The Caste? They continued bellowing their narrow narratives wherever they could, though their designs to thoroughly bend and break and mold and mould and demolish and destroy existing society to recreate a dogdom in their dogmatic images, however that might have appeared, were ultimately tempered or distempered. Partially based on Rat Dog's persistent insistence, and partially because lowly canines were simply tired of doing nothing else but lying around the place, dogdom's bowsers finally dug up enough gumption to counter the more radical viewpoints with equally influential packs that pushed their own interests with similar fervor, energy, and effort. This eventually balanced out the imbalances and got all dogs on a better path.

REFERENCES

Use these search terms to discover more information on relevant technologies.

Human Regeneration, Longevity Science, Longevity Diet, Longevity Genes, Aging and Age Engineering, Ageing, Regenerative Medicine, Senescent Cells, Biogerontology, Anti-Aging Movement, Lifespans, Health and Life Extension, Aging Treatments, Reverse Aging

ABOUT THE AUTHOR

Blade Cort writes Age Engineering and Longevity Science Fiction as well as Genetic Engineering Science Fiction novels and plays that are mercilessly littered with pedantic discourse, pointless diatribes, and persistent droning about humanity's pervasive derelictions. The pulp drivel exhumed from his keyboard is as terrifying and graceless as overcooked cafeteria peas. Visit https://www.bladecort.com.

www.ingramcontent.com/pod-product-compliance
Lightning Source LLC
Chambersburg PA
CBHW031626210526
45464CB00004B/1777